Mind, Set, and Match

Linda K. Bunker is director of Motor Learning and chairperson of the Department of Physical Education at the University of Virginia.

Robert J. Rotella is director of Sport Psychology at the University of Virginia.

They are the co-authors of several articles and books, including *Mind Mastery for Winning Golf*, published by Prentice-Hall. Both authors are active and successful tennis players who have served as consultants to many other players.

Mind, Set, and Match

USING YOUR HEAD TO PLAY BETTER TENNIS

LINDA K. BUNKER
ROBERT J. ROTELLA

Prentice-Hall, Inc., Englewood Cliffs, New Jersey 07632

Library of Congress Cataloging in Publication Data

Bunker, Linda K.

Mind, set, and match.

"A Spectrum Book."

Includes index.

1. Tennis—Psychological aspects. I. Rotella, Robert. II. Title.

GV1002.9.P75B86 1982 796.342'2 82-9113
ISBN 0-13-583484-8 AACR2
ISBN 0-13-583476-7 (pbk.)

A SPECTRUM BOOK.

Illustrations by *Marc R. Wakat and Philip Scavo*
Cover design by *Mary Zeldin*
Manufacturing buyer: *Cathie Lenard*

10 9 8 7 6 5 4 3 2 1

Printed in the United States of America

This Spectrum Book can be made available to businesses and organizations at a special discount when ordered in large quantities. For more information, contact: Prentice-Hall, Inc., General Publishing Division, Special Sales, Englewood Cliffs, New Jersey 07632.

ISBN 0-13-583484-8

ISBN 0-13-583476-7 {PBK}

Prentice-Hall International, Inc., *London*
Prentice-Hall of Australia Pty. Limited, *Sydney*
Prentice-Hall Canada Inc., *Toronto*
Prentice-Hall of India Private Limited, *New Delhi*
Prentice-Hall of Japan, Inc., *Tokyo*
Prentice-Hall of Southeast Asia Pte. Ltd., *Singapore*
Whitehall Books Limited, *Wellington, New Zealand*

Dedicated to Francis "Tony" Bunker, whose fatherly love and teaching led me to realize the joys and challenges of tennis, and to Billie Bunker, whose motherly patience, love, and understanding allowed me to pursue success and happiness in every endeavor.

LINDA

And to Darlene, who spent endless hours practicing and playing with me, to John Billing, my first teacher and practice partner, and to Nick and Flora Tomasetti, for all of the great moments we've shared on the court.

BOB

Contents

Foreword

I have enjoyed tennis as a player, teacher, and promoter for many years. During this time tennis has become an immensely popular social, recreational, and competitive sport on a worldwide basis.

Over the years, in instructional programs conducted by 4-Star Tennis Academy and the U.S. Professional Tennis Association I have taught and worked with tennis players at every ability level, helping them to improve their play and reach their full tennis potential. Often the greatest obstacle to achieving these goals is the player's inability to master the mental aspects of the game. Many players often seem to fall apart in competitive situations and play much worse than in practice sessions.

Mind, Set, and Match is a book that will be extremely beneficial to teachers, coaches, and players of all levels. It will aid in developing a mastery of the game's mental aspects. The book shows that by controlling your mind you not only can play better tennis, but also enjoy it more.

In the past most tennis books have treated the mental and physical aspects of tennis as separate entities. *Mind, Set, and Match* teaches the importance of combining mental and physical training to achieve optimal performance. A detailed approach is provided to assure that you can effectively practice the whole game of tennis.

This book shows the player how to develop realistic goals and attain them. It shows how to develop confidence and concentration. You will learn important relaxation techniques to help eliminate inappropriate muscle tension. The authors also provide excellent advice on how to get the most out of your lessons and practice sessions.

I highly recommend that people of all ages read and use this book to help them enjoy a lifetime of tennis.

MIKE EIKENBERRY
Director,
4-Star Tennis Academy

Preface

Tennis is a game that has brought great joy to many people. It provides both a difficult and exciting challenge—challenge requiring that each serious player set his or her mind to mastering the game, thus the title *Mind, Set, and Match.*

Many tennis books have attempted to help players improve their games through improved stroke mechanics. In recent years a number of books have appeared on the market that have suggested that all learning and performance problems are caused by mental errors. Some have even indicated that playing tennis is easy and natural.

Mind, Set, and Match presents a departure from previous approaches. It uses information developed in the field of sport psychology to show you an effective approach for attaining your tennis-playing potential. Although this book is psychological in its orientation, emphasis is placed on the interaction between the psychological and physical aspects of tennis. A detailed and systematic approach for combining the mind and body is presented. Sections contain self-assessment inventories to help you increase your self-awareness and to allow you to better use the information presented in each chapter.

This book provides a realistic view of what it takes to become a successful tennis player. Tennis is a difficult game, and performing in competition can be challenging. You must read and comprehend the book so that you will be able to understand yourself and the mental and physical demands of tennis. Then the real fun begins. You can put forth the effort and self-discipline necessary to allow yourself to perform up to your potential.

The approach has been effective for many others, and it will work for you if you will be patient and persistent. Give yourself the opportunity to excel. You deserve it.

Acknowledgments

We wish to acknowledge the influence on our tennis thinking and playing of various persons who have stimulated our interests and motivated us to understand the game. In particular, our parents, Billie and Francis ("Tony") Bunker, and Laura and Guido Rotella; the inspirers and scholars of tennis, Maureen Connelly Brinker, Eve Kraft, John Conroy, Mary Willson Pinder, Mary Slaughter, C. Alphonso Smith, Mike Dolan, Dennis Van der Meer, Phil Rogers; and to all the children and adults we have had the opportunity to teach, especially John, Pat, and Gabriela. Our appreciation is also extended to Marc Wakat and Philip Scavo for their creative and artistic contributions and to Guy Rotella for his editorial assistance. The contributions of D. H. Meichenbaum, R. Nideffer, and D. M. Ronan to sport psychology and to our thinking must also be acknowledged.

Of particular significance in each of our lives has been the support and encouragement provided by Darlene and Diane. Their positive attitudes and patience as we were writing *Mind, Set, and Match* were most helpful.

1

Do You Really Want to Be Successful?

Individuals who want to succeed at tennis must understand what motivates them to compete in the first place. Motivational differences frequently separate the champion from the mediocre or average player. With the exception of extremely gifted athletes, success in a sport such as tennis requires a moderate to high level of achievement motivation.

Tennis players who lack high levels of achievement motivation but who wish to improve their games must change their motivational tendencies. Fortunately, one's level of achievement motivation, one's desire to meet standards of excellence, *can* be modified. The first step is to understand what you value and to be more aware of your own attitudes toward tennis.

The Tennis Attitude and Motivation Profile (TAMP) that follows is designed to help you determine if you are a high- or low-achievement-motivated tennis player. The TAMP is intended to help you. Be honest with yourself as you answer each question or your profile will be inaccurate and of little value. Do not consider the TAMP a "test." It is, rather, a tool to improve self-awareness and to help make low achievers more receptive to a change in their motivational level.

Before reading further, get a pencil, read the instructions, complete the Tennis Attitude and Motivation Profile, and score your profile according to the procedures detailed at the end of the profile. This book will be of greatest value to you if you fill in the TAMP before reading the rest of the material—*so do it now.*

TAMP: TENNIS ATTITUDE AND MOTIVATION PROFILE

Instructions: This inventory is designed to evaluate your responses to situations relevant to attaining your potential in tennis. The intention of the inventory is to help you become more aware of how your own behavior and thoughts hinder your chances of attaining your potential as a tennis player.

To get the most out of the inventory, answer each question in the manner that most accurately describes your feelings. Do not try to fool the inventory. You will only be fooling yourself and decreasing your chances of benefiting from this self-awareness questionnaire.

After reading each question, circle the number under the answer which best describes your behavior.

	Strongly Agree	*Mildly Agree*	*Mildly Disagree*	*Strongly Disagree*
1. While playing competitive tennis, I concentrate totally on my game rather than spending my time and attention socializing with other tennis players.	4	3	2	1
2. In a tennis tournament I prefer to compete against opponents who play at approximately the same level as I do, rather than against opponents who are not nearly as good as I am.	4	3	2	1
3. I spend most of my practice time on the shots at which I am good.	1	2	3	4
4. I think about my future tennis performance rather than past performances.	4	3	2	1
5. I work (practice, play, think about, read) year-round in order to be successful in tennis.	4	3	2	1

	Strongly Agree	*Mildly Agree*	*Mildly Disagree*	*Strongly Disagree*
6. I would rather play an average or poor tennis match and win than play well and lose.	1	2	3	4
7. Even though there are weaknesses in my game, I would rather continue playing as I am at the present time than to make changes in my strokes which are not likely to dramatically improve my game for at least three months.	1	2	3	4
8. I prefer to read a well-written informative book on tennis than watch a good movie.	4	3	2	1
9. I find that I am constantly comparing my tennis game to those of other tennis players.	1	2	3	4
10. I often worry that I will never improve my tennis game.	1	2	3	4
11. I find that my interest in tennis and desire to play change frequently.	1	2	3	4
12. If I had trouble serving a topspin serve, I would keep practicing and using it rather than regularly switching to a flat, push serve.	4	3	2	1
13. I enjoy trying to learn shots which other tennis players find difficult.	4	3	2	1
14. I try to play my best even though I know my opponent is better than I am.	4	3	2	1
15. I do not spend much time practicing my overhead because I do not find it very enjoyable or exciting.	1	2	3	4
16. I do not feel that I am as mentally tough as most of the tennis players I play against.	1	2	3	4

	Strongly Agree	*Mildly Agree*	*Mildly Disagree*	*Strongly Disagree*
17. When I lose in a tournament I take it hard and it bothers me for several days.	1	2	3	4
18. If I have played poorly in a tournament, I spend *most* of my practice time for the next weeks on the shots that I hit poorly during the tournament.	4	3	2	1
19. I find that I spend more time practicing and drilling than other tennis players.	4	3	2	1
20. I am often self-conscious when people watch me play tennis.	1	2	3	4
21. I believe that I have the ability to be a much better player than I presently am, and that effective practice will pay off.	4	3	2	1
22. I feel that I frequently play poorly because I am unlucky.	1	2	3	4
23. I think that a good tennis game is something that you are born with rather than something you can develop.	1	2	3	4
24. I sometimes fail to practice so that I have an excuse for not playing well.	1	2	3	4
25. Tennis is *too* important to me and sometimes I try *too* hard to do well.	1	2	3	4

Scoring the TAMP: To determine your score on the TAMP, simply add up the total of all of the numbers that you have circled.

Maximum Score = 100 My Total Score ______

Zone	*Score*	
A	100–90	Potential Maximizer
B	89–70	Above Average Potential Maximizer
C	69–50	Average Potential Attainment
D	49–35	Below Average Potential Maximizer
E	34–25	Potential Minimizer

Scoring and Interpreting the TAMP: The TAMP was developed as a practical tool to help tennis players increase their self-awareness of personal attitudes which may affect their ability to attain their potential in tennis. The profile has been designed to be useful for both male and female tennis players of various ages. Some of the items were written so that a positive response indicates that the motive to approach success (which describes the high achiever) is greater than the motive to avoid failure (which describes the low achievers). Some items were written in the opposite direction.

This inventory was not designed to identify winners and losers. The intent is to help you recognize whether or not you are approaching tennis as effectively as possible. You may discover that your past attitudes and practice strategies have not allowed you to become the best tennis player you can be. The remainder of this book is intended to be especially useful to those tennis players who know that they can be better, to those whose TAMP scores indicate that they tend to be minimizers and to those who wish to become greater maximizers. This book is designed to make you a more successful tennis player (1) by helping you to understand the advantages and/or disadvantages of your motivational tendencies, (2) by helping you to modify these tendencies when need be, and consequently (3) by modifying your behavior.

HIGH- VS. LOW-ACHIEVEMENT-MOTIVATED TENNIS PLAYERS (MAXIMIZERS VS. MINIMIZERS)

Sport psychologists interested in personality variables have identified characteristics of individuals with high and low achievement motivations. High achievers (maximizers) score 80 or above on the TAMP and are individuals who prefer competitive situations in which they have approximately a 50–50 chance of success. They set realistic goals, and are more interested in future performances than present or past performances. Maximizers also have a great deal of perseverance. They tend to remember more of their weaknesses than strengths following competitive situations.

In contrast, low achievers (minimizers) are individuals who prefer extremely easy or extremely difficult tasks and are more interested in immediate or present performances than in past or future performances. They are less likely to persevere and tend to remember more of their strengths than their weaknesses following competitive situations.

The role of causal attributions for success or failure in achievement situations must be understood. As a result of their goal-setting preference, maximizers attribute success to internal factors such as ability and effort, and failure to either bad luck or lack of effort. When they attribute failure to lack of effort, the result is an increase in motivation and effort in the future. Practice sessions become more meaningful because full confidence remains in their own abilities.

Minimizers typically prefer to set either extremely low or extremely high goals. The setting of extremely low goals creates situations in which success comes so easily that it can be attributed to the ease of the task. The setting of extremely high goals creates situations in which success is so unlikely that, if it occurs, the player is likely to attribute it to external factors such as luck rather than internal factors such as ability or effort. The result is that low-achievement-motivated tennis players typically display a self-concept reflecting a perception of lack of ability combined with a tendency to actively circumvent failure and/or worry about failure disproportionately.

It becomes increasingly apparent that high-achievement-motivated players take credit for success and will simply work harder when faced with failure. Low-achievement-motivated players do just the opposite. They create situations that minimize their personal responsibility for success, and yet they blame their failures on lack of ability rather than lack of effort.

In summary, the interpretation of success or failure varies in high- and low-achievement-motivated tennis players. Low-achievement-motivated players perceive failure as the result of innate ability. High-achievement-motivated tennis players perceive failure as the result of a lack of effort. Clearly, the effort one expends can be modified. Natural ability, on the other hand, may be more permanent. Clearly, physical attributes such as strength, flexibility, coordination, timing, and tension management can be modified if you wish to attain your potential. Obviously, the low achiever digs a hole that gets deeper and deeper. Even under comparable conditions, tennis players with high achievement motivation blame themselves more for their failures than credit themselves for their successes. Thus it matters not "whether you win or lose" but "where you place the blame."

It should be emphasized that there is absolutely nothing wrong with being a minimizer or low achiever in tennis. As a matter of fact, you may even enjoy your game and have more fun as a result of playing with such an approach. However, if you are only playing for fun and have no desire to be a high achiever, do not become frustrated when you do not consistently win. Recognize that you cannot be a success without effort and self-confidence in your ability.

ARE YOUR PERCEPTIONS ACCURATE?

Do you make accurate attributions about your explanations of success or failure? Each tennis player must assess his own skills and feelings about competence in a careful manner.

For example, it may happen that you hit short lobs all day and still win a tennis match. If this happens to you and you inaccurately perceive that you have a great lob, you are likely to get into trouble on the court when you run into a player who is a little better than your last opponent. If he can hit an overhead, you may be beaten by your own short lobs. So be sure that you are honest and accurate in evaluating your wins and your performances. Be happy about your success but know that during your practice sessions you must develop a deeper lob.

Perceptual errors of the sort described above frequently occur when you win despite not having any depth on your groundstrokes or pace and control on your second serves. If you win because you played a weaker opponent, you must assess your performance relative to the level of play that you wish to attain rather than the one you've attained already.

In a similar fashion, if you play as well as you can possibly play, but lose to a far superior player, you must focus on your execution of *your* game. Don't be disappointed or discouraged just because you lost.

On the other hand, if your goals include playing at the level of the opponent who just beat you, you must reevaluate your game. Determine which parts of your game must be changed in order to enable you to advance to the next level. Do not decide that you are terrible and simply give up trying.

One way to determine if your perceptions are accurate is to get help from a qualified professional. If you explain your goals in tennis, including the level of tennis to which you aspire, a professional teacher can help you evaluate your strengths and show you which of your strokes will break down in competition and how to change them.

This approach will only be useful to you if you are willing to admit your weaknesses and then work to correct them. Some players would rather decide that the pro is lacking in knowledge, patience, or insight and use this perception to provide an excuse for discarding the new information. Be certain to pick a knowledgeable professional and then accept the feedback you get.

You can also help yourself identify your own strengths and weaknesses. After you play your next competitive match ask yourself the following questions:

"Given a choice of shots, which would I rather be able to hit at match point?"

"Which shots fall apart most often during competition?"

"Which shots make me feel the most nervous or uncertain?"

The answers to these questions will indicate those shots at which you already are quite good and those that you need to practice. Now go to work and strive to improve them.

ADMIT AND ATTACK YOUR WEAKNESSES

Recognize that staying with your old strokes and your old game may indeed be comfortable, far more comfortable than a change will be. Most players unfortunately choose this feeling of comfort rather than striving for growth and improvement. As a result, their game stagnates. Soon they either get frustrated or quit because they inaccurately perceive that their problem is a lack of talent. They may grow more comfortable and happy with their level of play and continue without improving. This point is made not to criticize people who accept this approach. Rather it is made to explain why their play never improves. If you wish to get better, this comfortable feeling is quite ineffective. Indeed, it may be far easier to continue to serve with a forehand grip and without spin rather than to switch to serving with a backhand grip with spin, even though people are destroying your second serve. It may be easier to "push" backhand shots with a leading elbow rather than turning and stroking the ball more effectively.

Many players fail to learn how to serve and volley effectively. Yet the absence of this skill hinders performance, especially when playing doubles. Anyone can learn to serve and volley, especially in doubles where you must only cover half the court. But most players try it a few times, make errors, and decide it is impossible for them to learn. If you wish to learn, find a friend who would also like to learn and practice together. Be patient—it will take time. Constantly remind yourself that it will pay off in the future. When you get frustrated think about how good you will feel when you are finally able to serve and volley. Think about how learning will force you to develop your footwork and learn how to hit the overhead that you may never have had. It will be impossible to be bored as you learn these new skills. Your game will get better and better and you will enjoy tennis more and more.

WHOM YOU PLAY IN PRACTICE MAKES A DIFFERENCE

In choosing daily practice opponents you should be sure to consider your own desires for skill development as well as such matters as psychological compatibility. For instance, should your opponent be better than you, weaker, or equal? The answer may be "one of each."

Better opponents are great for forcing your game to greater heights. The old adage that "you never get better playing weaker opponents" is certainly true. It may, however, be devastating to constantly subject yourself to competition much better than you are. The distinction here may be that whether competing or practicing try to be realistic about your opponents.

For beginners or young players, it may be that the choice of opponents should be based more on the psychological impact than on physical issues. For example, if success breeds success and achievement motivation, it may be better to compete against others of equal or less skill. But you must make certain that strokes are being developed which will hold up at the higher levels of competition. If you know that you have trouble playing left-handers, then instead of avoiding them make a point of setting up a regular match against a lefty. If you have trouble returning high-kicking serves, find someone to play who has a kick serve. Do you tend to lose your patience in tournament matches? Then start playing more opponents who can keep the ball in play "all day long."

The idea here is rather obvious. Don't run away from the very problems that are keeping you from improving. Be honest with yourself. Admit these weaknesses and find practice partners who will force you to improve. Playing against opponents whom you feel comfortable with will not enable you to maximize your potential. Instead, it will leave you forever feeling uncomfortable against certain tournament opponents.

Consider, for a moment, the potential "costs" of competing in the following pairing—a child 16 years old versus an adult. The child has little to lose. Because of his age, the expectancy for success would be less, so if he loses, it's OK, and if he wins, it's great! On the other hand, the adult has much more to lose, unless of course the players are realistic about relative ability levels and what may be generated from the experience.

SO YOU WANT TO BE A CHAMPION!

If you want to be a champion, you may in fact be saying that you want to be different. You want to stand out. You love this game of tennis and you'd like to master it. You like the idea of being respected for being dedicated to improving your game.

Watch out! Many others have felt just like you. Most of them get discouraged and lose their enthusiasm. There will be many frustrations and many obstacles. There will be great moments when you may love tennis and yourself. But there may also be many disappointments. You may question your dedication and commitment. You may find yourself saying that tennis is a waste of time, or a dumb and unfair game.

When you are happy and excited about your progress, your emotions can be a great source of motivation. But when you are having problems, your feelings can really work against your continued motivation. You must learn to use emotions to help you when they are useful and block them out when they can hinder your continued improvement.

Being good and feeling on top of your tennis world can be a lot of fun. But getting there may not be if you are not careful. You must learn to love and enjoy a solid challenge. You must look forward to overcoming disappointments.

It is not always easy to stick to a commitment to improvement in tennis. There will be many distractions. They will be particularly difficult to cope with if winning does not come to you early. When you are attaining success regularly, it is easy to work hard on the tennis court. You will enjoy being there. Friends will praise and admire you. Others will try to emulate you. But when your game is at a standstill, your mind will often question your dedication. People who don't understand may constantly ask why you put so much into tennis when you seemingly get so little back. When this happens, you must fight the natural tendency of your mind and your ego to protect you.

You must talk yourself into continuing your practice. You must continue your persistence. Recognize that it is during these difficult times that most people quit. Those who continue to improve are the ones who have been able to maintain their persistence even in the toughest of times.

Anyone can give up and spend his time sleeping or sitting by the side of the swimming pool. Certainly it is all right to do so. It is even quite comfortable. There is no risk involved in doing so. But if you wish to be better at tennis and prefer to be different, you will have to think differently. You must take pride in being a good player and assume that others will respect you and perhaps even imitate you if you stick to your plan.

Be alert to thinking patterns which can undermine your motivation. Catch them and stop them before they spread. It will

Enjoy your new dedication to tennis. Believe in yourself and your ability to improve.

ultimately be up to you. It is your mind. You can either control it so that you can attain your goals or let it control you and allow you to give in. You can be sure that when you are ready to give up, many others will be there with open arms to welcome you. They would love to have you be just like them. You and you alone must decide which you want to be.

Are you exceptionally talented? It can be a definite advantage to be blessed with exceptional athletic ability. But often such talent is wasted. Talent has its hazards if you are not careful and aware.

When you're talented, the game comes to you rapidly and easily. Unless you live in a community or belong to a club where there are a lot of talented athletes, winning may come too easily to you. You may get away with doing a lot of things wrong. You will get away with sloppy strokes, poor strategy, lazy footwork, or a lack of concentration against less gifted players. But you won't when you play others who have equal or nearly equal abilities. So if you wish to become the best you can be, constantly evaluate your game. Compare your skills to those players with talent. Make sure you constantly work in practice on improving and refining your skills.

A word of caution: Don't be a burnt-out perfectionist! As previously stated, a high level of achievement motivation is most crucial to success in tennis. However, it is indeed possible to be so highly motivated and so greatly in need of success that you can work against yourself.

Be cautious of becoming so concerned with your tennis success that it controls *you*, rather than you controlling it. Do not allow yourself to become so driven that you are constantly overpracticing and thus becoming overtired and unable physically or mentally to practice effectively.

Strive for success, but don't become such a perfectionist that you can never think of anything else. People who do will often "burn out" and lose their motivation before they ever attain their goals.

Do you tend to believe that if you fail to become a "super" tennis player, you will be a second-rate person?

Do you believe that if you can't play tennis really well, there is no point in playing at all?

Do you find it embarrassing to make errors?

Would you find it shameful to display weaknesses or foolish behavior?

Are average performances unsatisfying to you?

If your response to all or most of these questions is a resounding yes, you may be such a perfectionist that you will not be able to perform as well as you like. The common tendency is to think that perfectionism will lead to success. But often it is an attitude that may stand in the way of success.

You must strive for balance. Do not settle for haphazard and ineffective performance, but don't strive for instant perfection either.

Perfectionists too often set unrealistically high goals. They will tend to measure their entire self-worth in terms of wins and losses.

Such individuals often end up working against, rather than for, themselves. If you feel that your self-esteem is lowered when you fail, you may experience more anxiety and depression than is best for reaching your tennis potential.

In addition, the sense of rejection that so frequently follows failure may cause tennis players who are too perfectionistic to have interpersonal problems. They tend to react to failure with such frustration that others stay away from them, and eventually practice or playing partners are impossible to find. When this tendency is combined with a tendency to respond defensively to criticism they fail to receive helpful advice, or when they do get it, they fail to accept it.

When perfectionistic tennis players compete in doubles they often become annoyed if their partners don't share their desire. They spend a great deal of time attempting to find partners. Seldom are partners found who will make perfectionists happy.

Perfectionistic tennis players must learn to lower their standards or goals. They must strive to attain rational and realistic perspectives toward their goals in tennis. Yes, attaining success in tennis will require that you take your game seriously. You must set goals and strive to maximize your potential. But you must also retain the ability to laugh at yourself and enjoy playing.

Players who are perfectionists to the point that it is disadvantageous usually have a dichotomous thinking style. The player loses a match and thinks, "I'm a total failure. I'm terrible. All my practice is wasted." This thinking style causes the perfectionists to fear failure far more than it deserves to be feared, and as a result they overreact. Players with this inclination must learn to keep their experiences in perspective. Failure is not terrible. "It is a momentary setback." Hopefully, it taught you something about your game that will help you in the future. Practice was not wasted. Think where your game would be if you had not practiced.

A second thinking style that works against the success of the perfectionistic tennis player is the tendency to overgeneralize. When struggling to develop a backhand, this player concludes, "I'll never get this right. I'm always missing." This thinking style often undermines motivation and persistence. When motivation does continue the perfectionist is often so uptight and anxious about the possibility of not improving that he in fact can't improve. A vicious cycle is initiated which causes problems to be multiplied.

Perfectionistic players tend to also have a third thinking system that works against them. They frequently make use of "should," "ought," and "must" statements. Failure or errors tend to be followed by overly self-critical thoughts that decrease rather than increase effectiveness. They believe that they "*should* have won," "*ought to* do better," and "*must* be better." This thinking usually leads to the irrational thought that, if they don't do better, they will be total failures as tennis players and persons. The result is increased anxiety and depression. These mood states are antagonistic rather than beneficial to maximizing performance.

So strive for success. Set goals that are high and realistic. Go for it! But don't be such a perfectionist that you destroy yourself. This error is as damaging, if not more so, than being an underachiever who sets goals that are too low and also minimizes improvement. Keep in mind the motivational errors which occur when an extreme approach in either direction is followed. Use this knowledge to guide your plans for success.

PERFECTIONIST THINKING STYLES THAT HURT YOUR GAME

"I'm terrible" = fear of failure
"I'll never get it right" = overgeneralizing
"Should," "ought," and "must" syndrome = perfectionist tendencies

---

A MOTIVATIONAL PLAN FOR SUCCESS IN TENNIS

All tennis players desiring success must recognize the importance of believing in their ability and recognizing the important role that effort plays. You cannot deceive yourself into believing in your natural ability alone. The only way to gain self-confidence is to seek out your weaknesses and practice hard to eliminate them.

A minimal amount of physical ability is no doubt required for success in tennis. But witness many of the players on the professional tour, or those at your home courts, who are outstanding. They do not all possess a great deal more physical ability than you do, but perhaps some of them work more diligently or more systematically on their games.

If you are becoming increasingly aware that you have had motivational and perceptual weaknesses, deficits which have prevented you from achieving your potential in tennis, make a commitment to the program detailed in the following sections and you will be pleased with your improvement!

The first step in the program requires that you develop (in writing) a list of realistic goals for yourself in tennis. Both a list of long-range goals and a list of sequential short-range goals need to be carefully identified. This is a most important first step in becoming a maximizer or high achiever in tennis. Do not allow yourself to be lazy in the process. Be sure that each goal is objective and measurable so that your confidence will be able to naturally grow as you achieve each sequential goal on the way to achieving your long-range goal. By objectively detailing your improvement as a result of increased and organized effort, you will see your own real improvement.

It is important that tennis players realize that the attainment of these goals may require a great deal of effort. The major value of sequential short-range goals is to allow you to personally see your own progress in the development of your tennis game. Your goals should set you up for success rather than failure. For instance, do not decide that you wish to hit deep, wide serves each time if you are just developing a good, forceful service motion. Base your goals honestly on your desire to improve and the amount of effort you are willing to put forth. If your goal is to play like the club champion or a touring pro, be willing to take as many lessons and devote as many hours to practice as they have in developing their games. Look at yourself in comparison to others with whom you wish to compete. Are they ahead of you at the present? Do they have more talent than you, or have they been practicing for years? If the answer to any of the above is yes, then be ready to practice a lot more than you will see them practice. Accept this fact and be happy with it. Don't let it be a frustration to you. If you don't do this, you are being unrealistic, setting yourself up for failure, and in essence thinking like a minimizer. Be realistic. Understand that the quantity of practice is not the answer. You must have quality practice and you must concentrate and practice correctly.

Remember, low-achievement-motivated tennis players do not realize the value of setting small sequential goals in order to realize long-range ambitions. In order to really improve your tennis, long-range goals must be perceived as more valuable than immediate gratification. Far too often the low-achievement-motivated athlete never plans out how to attain a goal which is one to five years in the future. Consequently, minimizers with more talent will be surpassed by maximizers with less talent who work hard over extended time periods.

To make a tennis dream come true,
analyze your strengths and weaknesses.

BE OBJECTIVE: LIST YOUR STRENGTHS AND WEAKNESSES

The second step in your program requires that you draw up a master list of all of the tennis skills needed for reaching the desired level of proficiency (physical skills, strategy, rules, proper equipment, physical conditioning, mental training). The list should be very specific. With the help of a professional or a tennis-playing friend, detail in sequential order a list of your tennis skills starting with your weakest skill and working on up to your strongest skill. When this list has been completed, a specific amount of time should be allocated during each practice session for working on individual weaknesses only. As each weakness is alleviated and you reach your short-range goal, less practice time should be spent on it. Time is then increasingly spent on the next weakest skill. This process continues until you have accomplished all your short-range goals which will lead you to your long-range goals. At this point you should reevaluate your tennis game, search for your weaknesses again, and set new goals. (See Chapter 9 or the Appendix for a detailed approach to setting up this program.)

The minimizer or low-achievement-motivated tennis player tends to spend more time practicing strengths than weaknesses—especially when surrounded by friends or other players. Yet the best way to improve yourself in any endeavor is to constantly seek out your weaknesses and do whatever is necessary to remediate them. In assessing your weaknesses, it would be wise to determine which skills are most important to tennis success. For instance, you might take into account the fact that the game of tennis relies heavily on serving, returning serves, and hitting ground strokes. The relative contribution of these areas should all be considered when deciding which weaknesses are the most detrimental to your own tennis game.

In the future, when you play tennis poorly or lose a match, instead of losing confidence in your ability, look for your weaknesses and then do something to improve them. As you eliminate the number of weaknesses in your game, you will realize that you do have talent and that the right attitude toward practice does make a difference. The result will most likely be that you will have the confidence to achieve your goals in tennis. You will be on your way to becoming a high-achievement-motivated tennis player.

Remember, think about your weaknesses—actively seek them out—after competition, whether you win or lose. While playing, think positively about your strengths and be confident, because you are on your way to eliminating your weaknesses.

2
Building Confidence in Your Tennis Game

It is virtually impossible to find a champion tennis player who lacks self-confidence. Some may be very vocal in stating their confidence. Others may keep it to themselves or even verbally state to others that they aren't too good so as not to offend anyone or be considered a braggart. But in every case champions are filled with self-confidence.

Very often the only difference between the champion and many others is just this belief in their own ability. Sport psychologists often encounter athletes who have the ability to perform the desired skills or tasks but do not believe they have the ability.

How many times have you heard it said that a certain tennis player "plays like a winner" and that another "plays like a loser," or that if a certain player even realized how good she is, she would become a champion. Tennis is indeed referred to as a mental game.

It is amazing how little effort in the past has been dedicated to the development of the mind of a winner, when so much effort has been directed at developing the strokes and strategies of a winner. In recent years, techniques have been developed by sport psychologists for just this former purpose and have proven to be effective. Before detailing such techniques for you to use, let us explain their rationale so you will increase your awareness and understanding and therefore be more likely to utilize them regularly.

TENNIS SELF-CONCEPT

Your tennis self-concept is your personal conception of the kind of tennis player you are. This concept is the result of all your experiences as a player. Included in it are all your successes and failures, moments of pride and of shame, as well as feedback or comments made by friends, parents, coaches, instructors, opponents, and yourself. Unfortunately, with the exception of a few fortunate individuals, most players' tennis experiences may have been labeled as failures due to the emphasis in our society upon success early in life. If your early tennis experiences could have all been successful, there would be no problem with self-confidence.

Recognize right now and accept the fact that your tennis self-concept will not change overnight. But also realize that you can change it if you will make a commitment to the techniques described in this book. They have worked for many others, and they will work for you if you desire to discover your potential and are willing to practice the physical and mental aspects of your tennis game in order to attain it. The decision is yours.

PROGRAM YOURSELF FOR SUCCESS

Most tennis players have experienced a momentary loss of confidence. Many others can identify with a rather permanent lack of self-confidence in their tennis games. For most of these players, their games are very effective on the practice court or when competing against someone weaker. But place these players in situations where they are not so self-confident and their games rapidly deteriorate.

The negative effect of a lack of self-confidence is likely to be a lack of persistence in one's effort to become a successful tennis player. After all, why practice hard on the physical and mental aspects of tennis if you do not believe that by doing so you can become successful? Players without self-confidence are also those most likely to quit or lose their motivation when faced with failure. It has been consistently demonstrated that the more self-confident an individual is, the more active his or her efforts to achieve success will be.

The aspiring tennis player must understand the extent to which perceived ability will influence actual performance. For example, the ninety-nine-pound woman was able to raise the front end of her automobile in an emergency to save her trapped child because she never allowed a thought of self-doubt to cross her mind. She saw her trapped child and reacted, expecting to lift the car and save her child.

The confident tennis player expects to get her first serve in, hit deep cross-court drives, and put away overheads. The winning tennis player is quite clearly self-confident and needs little help. But the problem with so many players in that self-confidence varies drastically from moment to moment. Hit one or two bad shots and suddenly you are expecting to flub the next shot. A few more bad shots and you have lost your confidence. You are headed into a slump. You become distracted, you start thinking about the mechanics of the stroke instead of relaxing and hitting the ball, and you may even change an efficient stroke to one much less efficient. Now you really have problems and have reason to be losing confidence.

If you wish to become a consistently effective and confident tennis player, you must prepare in advance. Your preparation in self-confidence should include tying your goal setting program to your self-confidence training program on a regular basis. Before detailing a daily program that will help you, let's explain the most effective way of building self-confidence in your tennis game.

BECOMING SELF-CONFIDENT

You can decide to take personal responsibility for your level of confidence and accept the *fact* that *you can train yourself to become self-confident.* Self-confidence is reflective of both (1) being able to perform the desired skill and (2) believing that you have the ability to perform effectively in a variety of situations. Clearly, both physical and mental training are required. If you are sure that you are physically capable of executing shots during competition, but are failing to do so because of a lack of confidence in that ability, then you should direct your thought mainly to the mental training aspects of your game.

INCREASING SELF-AWARENESS

A first step toward increasing self-confidence is to be able to identify whether you are confident or anxious during competition. A very simple and yet effective method of assessing anxiety in tennis is to become more self-aware of your thinking style. Because anxiety is a psychological state, your thinking as well as your physiological responses will tell you a great deal about whether or not you're anxious or self-confident. Following your next important tennis match, sit down in a quiet place and answer the following questions as honestly as possible:

1. *What* were your thoughts about yourself the day before the match? Did you fully expect to win or play well? Did you often have negative thoughts cross your mind? Were you worried about a particular shot that had given you trouble in the past? Did you worry that the wind would be blowing and you would play poorly? Did you fear that your serve or overhead would fail you?

   (Write down your thoughts as you remember them. The anxious thoughts suggest that you need to spend more time in the future on both physical and mental practice on those aspects of your game. If you lacked confidence, more needs to be done with your self-efficacy training.)
2. *When* did you feel the most anxious? Before the first game, or before your first serve? After double-faulting? Were you postive that you could recover, or did you question your ability to do so? What did you say to yourself prior to the overhead you missed at match point? Did you worry about missing it? Were you wondering what your friends or partner would think if you missed?

CAPITALIZE ON YOUR STRENGTHS AND ON OPPONENTS' WEAKNESSES

Average players are very confident of their strengths (usually the forehand) and cautious and emotional about their weaknesses (perhaps the backhand or overhand). Bearing this in mind, you will recognize that average players may cringe instinctively when a ball comes on the backhand side, and think something to themselves like, "Oh no, not another backhand!"

Don't let your mind become a tape recorder of bedlam—of whimpers, cries, and fears. Does your voice say, "You're going to lose" or "Watch the ball, dummy, bend your knees, racket back, head down, feet moving, finish high. . ."? Or worse yet, is there a voice yelling, "Why are you doing this? Quit. Get it over with."? The result of all this cacophony is that your body will probably forget all the tennis it ever knew!

In contrast, the positive voice in your mind does not always help. Have you ever been up 5–3 in the second set, serving, and thinking about winning—only to double-fault twice? The next thing you know it's 6–5 and you're still thinking of a victory. Then it's 4–2 in the tie-breaker, with three serves to win.

If during the match your mind becomes overloaded with the glorious images of a winner you may be distracted from the game itself. Your mental picture of fluid strokes, quicksilver movements, and point-winning overheads may interfere with your game-winning attention.

MENTAL REHEARSAL: WINNERS SEE WHAT THEY WANT TO HAPPEN; LOSERS SEE WHAT THEY FEAR MIGHT HAPPEN

It is well known that tennis players use mental rehearsal both on and off the tennis court. Martina Navratilova, Tracy Austin, and Bjorn Borg, as well as the duffer completely lacking in self-confidence, use mental rehearsal. The difference is in the picture. Confident tennis players have clear pictures or feelings of themselves executing the shot perfectly, or at least effectively. The player lacking in confidence imagines an ineffective result and because of the related anxiety fails to produce a clear picture. Furthermore, many tennis players lacking in confidence are unable to control their mental pictures at all. When these players practice mentally, they hit the ball out of bounds rather than straight, or swing quickly rather than smoothly. It appears that these problems are anxiety-related. If you find these problems occurring when you rehearse mentally, you must practice inducing relaxation prior to your mental practice as outlined in Chapter 6. With relaxation and regular practice, you will soon develop control over your mental rehearsal and be on the way to developing the mind of a self-confident winner.

If you know that your tennis strokes are already developed and that your head fails you during competition, give special attention to mental practice strategies for enhancing confidence. But if you also "know" you don't have the strokes, both physical and mental practice will be crucial to enhancing your confidence during competition.

IMAGERY

If you wish to be a consistent and efficient tennis player, you must realize that your body will do what you instruct it to do. But you must learn how to communicate with it.

The programming of success in sport through the use of the imagination has been gaining in popularity and utility since it was first introduced by Dr. Maxwell Maltz in his book *Psycho-Cybernetics* and followed up by Tim Galloway's *Inner Tennis*. Many professional tennis players as well as highly motivated athletes in other sports have benefited from the use of related techniques.

Our bodies learn and react similarly to both actual and imagined experiences. If you have ever walked down a dark, deserted street in a strange town and suddenly been startled by a noise or if you have ever awakened in the night from a bad dream, you are well aware that your body reacts emotionally and physiologically as if the imagined threats were real. You are scared. Likewise, if you sit on your back porch and close your eyes and imagine hitting a beautiful topspin serve, your body responds by relaxing. Your muscles learn from this kind of practice because they are stimulated by messages sent by the brain. The difference between this mental rehearsal and physical practice is that the stimulation is below the threshold level required for actual muscle movement.

Years of research and application have consistently detailed the important role of combining visualization with physical practice to build self-confidence in one's ability to perform successfully. Billie Jean King has often spoken of replaying her matches in her head while showering after play and correcting all errors. Some players replay specific shots *perfectly* before going to sleep at night after a match—a most effective technique for preparing for confidence in the future as well as getting into a relaxed and confident frame of mind. Recognize that this is far different from agonizing about mistakes prior to going to sleep.

The moment that an experience or belief about yourself enters your mind and forms a picture, it becomes subjectively true. It does not matter whether or not it is. You will perform on the tennis court as you picture yourself performing. Picture yourself double-faulting and chances are that you will lose confidence. Imagine missing a critical drop shot and you'll tighten up and most likely miss it! Picture successful shots and you will have made a major step in the right direction—you will have begun to program yourself for success.

Make a Self-Instruction Audio Tape

One of the easiest and most helpful things that you can do for your self-confidence is to put together your own tape program. Play the tapes over and over each night to let the good thoughts sink into your head.

An example from a tape program designed for a young female tennis player follows. Make your own tape based on this model and listen to it each night before you go to sleep.

> Here I am at the Center Court Racquet Club waiting for my match to be called. I am calm, I am good today, I feel very good. I observe my competition, they look good but I am better; they look strong, but I am stronger. My name is called; I see my opponent; she is tough, but I'm tougher. I open the can of balls and walk back to my side of the court. My opponent is nervous; I am calm. A grin appears as I consider her fear and my confidence. I loosen up and the adrenaline begins to flow. My feet are bouncing, waiting for a shot. I hit it out in front of me and it is a crisp deep shot.
>
> I hit my backhand with my knees bent, weight forward, and with topspin. My shots are aggressive but controlled. I'm rallying consistently and moving all over the court but not getting too close to the balls.
>
> I'm hitting all my groundstrokes with bent knees and topspin. I'm seeing all the impacts; I hit short shots perfectly with my eye on the ball, and I am down till the ball has bounced away for a winner on the other side.
>
> I am hitting very well; I hit my volleys in front of me, with a firm wrist, putting them away in the corners.
>
> I hit my overheads perfectly with my feet in position, reaching up to the ball, with my eyes on the ball until after the impact.
>
> I easily put them away in alternate corners. I now take my serves; I toss the ball just where I want it; the hit is with spin and it dives to a corner.
>
> Most of my serves go in, unreturnable, but a few miss by inches.
>
> My opponent says she is ready, but she isn't. I am confident that I can win, because my strokes and my mind are better. I win the toss but let her serve because losing the first game she serves will make her lose any confidence she had, and I will be that much more confident.
>
> She bounces the ball to begin serving; my muscles tense up in anticipation. I'm ready to spring in the direction of the ball. I return

the serve; I hit it to her backhand; I hit it again, and again, and again, until she misses; I am so patient.

I am playing well, with much intensity and much patience.

It is my turn to serve, I am very confident about my serve. I hit the first serve long; I bounce the ball with calm, deliberate determination.

I serve it and it is a good, clean, deep serve. I serve all my serves deep and consistently. My energy is overflowing; I can hit the ball all day with controlled aggression. I can move my opponent anywhere and hit it one time more than she can.

I have won the first set.

I give everything I've got to the second set.

I let nothing upset me.

I am in control of my mind and the ball.

My confidence is building; I am good and I can win.

I play one shot at a time the best that I can hit each ball.

The match is within my grasp, and I lose my concentration a little. But I think only of the ball, I just hit the ball in front, with my knees bent and my eyes on the ball.

I have got it back, I am in control again and I win my match.

As I walk off the court I am very confident, very strong, and very good.

I am a Winner.

I greet my opponent. I am courteous. Now is not the time to act confident. Be friendly. Help my opponent to feel better.

Visual Imagery to Understand Tennis Concepts

Each new practice strategy should include the use of both mental and physical practice. The old adage that a picture is often worth a thousand words may certainly be true. For example, many pros use the visual analogy of "brushing" over a tennis ball in order to produce a topspin. Why not suggest to yourself that a hand has been painted on the racket face so that the low-to-high stroke pattern will be produced. If you will simply take your racket back lower than usual and finish higher, you will brush the ball into a natural topspin. The amount of topspin will depend on how hard you hit the ball and how rapidly your racket is moving upward at contact. This topspin will allow you to hit the ball harder since it will drop into the court as a result of the spin. Notice how the visual image will help you practice this skill.

Imagery can also help you hit a slice or underspin. For example, Arthur Ashe has suggested that everyone's bread-and-butter backhand should be the slice or underspin shot. Acquiring the concept of this shot may be quite difficult. Let your visual imagery help. The motion required for a slice is the opposite of a topspin, with the racket starting high and coming through in a downward direction. The visual analogy would be to slice the back off the ball in order to put underspin on it. This shot will go lower over the net and bounce only slightly.

Visualize ball hit with topspin rotating toward the receiver, traveling higher over the net, dropping sharply, and bouncing higher. Backspin, slice, or underspin cause the ball to travel lower and bounce lower.

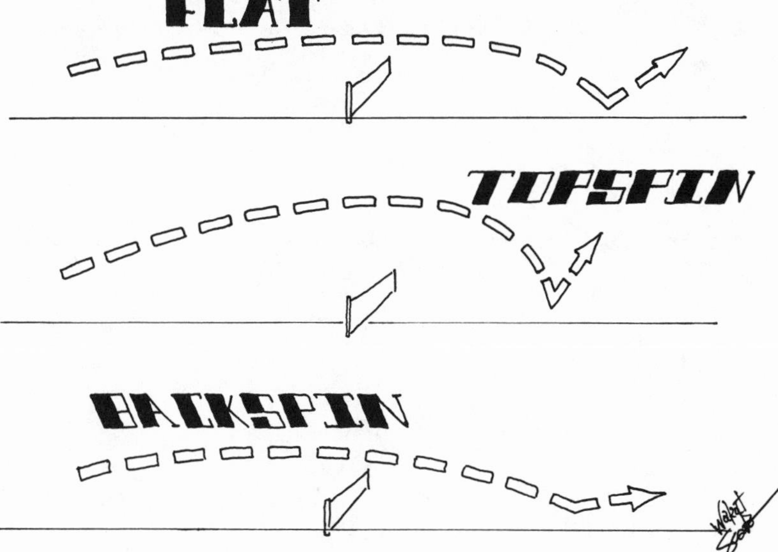

Visual imagery can also help you gain both a physical and mental "feel" for such things as the effect of ball spin on your shots. The spin refers to the rotation of the ball as it flies through the air. Most beginners hit the ball flat with little or no spin so that the ball travels through the air in a smooth arc as though it had been shot from a gun.

A ball hit with topspin—that is, a ball that rotates away from the hitter and toward the receiver—will drop more sharply and bounce higher than a flat ball. Imagine the forehands of hard hitters like Bjorn Borg and Martina Navratilova who use topspin to make sure the ball drops well inside the baseline yet bounces high enough to provide a difficult target for the receiver.

On the other hand, your image of a ball hit with underspin (so the underside of the ball rotates backward toward you) should show a ball which comes down slowly, almost floating through the air. On many surfaces, an underspin ball will skid and as a result bounce lower than a ball hit without spin, which may prevent your opponent from attacking.

Another good example of effective visual imagery might involve the backswing position on the serve. In order to provide appropriate leverage for the serve, the racket should be vis-

Visual imagery may help key certain concepts. On the serve, imagine your elbow high enough to remove an arrow from a quiver.

ualized as an arrow being withdrawn from a quiver. This image should emphasize the high elbow and upward extension of the arm. At the top of the serve motion, the racket (arrow) should be cocked forward-downward by a snap of the wrist, as if to hit someone on the top of the head.

Types of Visual Imagery: External and Internal

Your mental practice should include a variety of techniques on a regular basis. One type is known as external imagery and consists of a visually imagined experience of yourself executing various shots perfectly. Imagine watching yourself play each shot perfectly—just the way you planned it. In this exercise it is best to imagine shots that you are currently practicing physically. If you are about to play in a tournament, make a plan and then picture yourself playing the match according to your plan. Picture any bad situation you might get into, and imagine successfully overcoming it. Plan your strategy and imagine yourself successfully using it. Imagine yourself getting down 0–3 and coming back and winning the first set. Imagine double-faulting three times in a row and keeping your composure and then hitting great serves the rest of the match. Imagine losing the first set. What will your game plan be? Will you continue with the same strategy you used in the first set, or do you have an alternate plan? These thoughts tend to produce some anxiety. But these situations happen even to the best of players. You must learn to prepare for them or else you will have little confidence when you face them. When this happens, your mind, and thus your game, will likely fall apart. We suggest that you end this sort of "coping" mental practice at least two days before the start of the tournament. Use only positive pictures on the last days. Fill yourself with confident thoughts.

The second type of imagery that you should practice on a regular basis is known as internal imagery. It involves a proprioceptive or "feeling" practice frequently mentioned by top players. Feel your grip, feel your backswing begin and stop, feel your weight transfer through ball contact, feel yourself hit through the ball and finish.

You should analyze your swing and practice developing this "feel" so that you will be able to reproduce both a visual and a proprioceptive feel. Both are crucial to becoming a successful tennis player. Both internal and external rehearsal can be learned if you practice them regularly and combine them with physical practice. This is no shortcut, though. Planning for success will take effort, but it will insure that your efforts will attain the desired result.

Your visual rehearsal should also include rehearsal of your strategy. If you decide that you are going to attack, picture yourself attacking successfully. If you decide to be cautious, visualize yourself playing safe. How long will you stay with your strategy? Picture yourself sticking with it or changing, given a certain situation. The key is to be prepared. Don't get anxious or in trouble and make a hasty change in strategy that will only hurt your play. Imagine your prematch routine, get to the court early, stretch, decide how long to warm up; imagine practicing forehands, backhands, volleys, overheads, etc. Imagine hitting a great first serve with all friends and competitors watching. Imagine feeling great and playing great. Use this same routine in practice or on a daily basis.

Your mental rehearsal should center around the areas of desired improvement. Review your last tennis lesson, or the last time you hit a great shot. Visualize yourself doing the movements and mentally experience the feeling of accomplishment. Picture the rhythmic *tempo* of the stroke—the easy backswing and the solid hit through the ball to a balanced finish. Then, when you actually play, you will be able to step into each ball with confidence since you have executed a good stroke many times before in your mind.

The important role of confidence in getting prepared on the day before competition cannot be overestimated. You should practice only with those shots with which you may play well—work the "good stuff" into your system instead of trying to work the bad stuff out. This same approach should be applied to your mental practice on pretournament day.

After the tournament, continue your practice, review the shots that gave you trouble. Imagine yourself executing those shots smoothly and effectively each time. For example, plan your serves carefully. Don't just try to get the ball in, but see yourself placing it deep to the outside. Play one of your more difficult opponents in your mind. Carefully analyze a variety of shots. Visualize your approach shots and execute them well.

Mental rehearsal can be accomplished at almost any time of day—the time spent waiting for a client, the time spent at the beauty parlor, half-time at a football game, or during a TV commercial. Do not let your thoughts wander aimlessly—use those moments for some positive thinking about yourself and your game. It will improve your game as well as relax you.

The time between shots can also be used for effective practice. This spare time can be used to rehearse shots or contemplate strategy. Such practice is excellent because it prepares you for real-life events, and in fact acts as a dry run for your next shot.

While you are waiting for your opponent or partner, visualize yourself hitting various shots. See yourself executing the shot. Feel your body in its ready position, feel the backswing and forward swing to impact. Imagine yourself hitting a great volley or overhead smash.

Actual physical practice without hitting a ball can also be an effective use of this spare time. Practice tossing the ball as in the serve. Or swing your racket as if to mimic a powerful groundstroke. Emphasize those aspects which you have been practicing, such as the step forward and solid contact.

General conditioning and relaxation can also be enhanced between points. A few stretching exercises, toe touches, lateral bending, etc. can be very effective, not only for improving flexibility, but also to reduce undue tension and help you stay relaxed.

These techniques have been found to be the most effective and durable for improved tennis. Many others have been tried, but tend to be quite momentary. The strategies related to the mental side of tennis emphasized in this book *work* and will be permanent if practiced. You will be surprised when you actually get on the court how much confidence you have built up, and how much better your game is!

PRACTICE STRATEGY

Regular Practice:	Emphasize weaknesses
	Reinforce strengths
Pretournament:	Emphasize strengths
	Build confidence
Posttournament:	Review weaknesses
	Plan for future improvement

3
Attention and Distraction in Tennis

Many players are distracted by their own thoughts during a match. Distracting thoughts most typically tend to enter the mind on crucial points or when you are behind in a match.

Unfortunately, the mind tends to be very protective. If you let it, your mind will try to protect your ego. If you find yourself behind and you begin thinking, "I don't really care how I do" or "I could win if I wanted to," realize that these distracting thoughts are more for the purpose of protecting your ego in case you lose rather than of helping you concentrate and do your best.

The moment you find yourself playing point after point and trying to justify your failure, realize that you are probably not concentrating. When you start thinking "today is not my day," "I had a long, hard night," "I'm just too tired today," you are in trouble. This is not to say that these thoughts are not accurate. They very well may be. But dwelling on them while you are playing is not going to help you.

You would be much better off to realize before you start that you are tired. Decide upon an appropriate strategy for playing when you're tired. Then convince yourself not to use your problems as excuses. Use the match as a challenge to see if you can concentrate when you are tired or have other things on your mind.

If you are unable to concentrate, realize that you must improve on this skill. You could of course also decide to go to sleep earlier prior to your next match.

The thoughts that distract you can have an important influence on your concentration. Learn to control your mind in a way that will facilitate rather than hinder your motivation.

RECOGNIZE YOUR ATTENTION STYLE

Do you tend to "fly off the handle," "lose your cool," and get emotionally upset while playing tennis? If you do, you probably have a tendency to be *external* in your attentional style. Chances are that you frequently make impulsive decisions regarding shot selection. You will often make irrational and inappropriate decisions. Seldom will you stick to a game plan even if it has been carefully thought out. You may react emotionally to bad breaks—or fail to realize that bad breaks will even out, so you might as well forget about them. You would be much better off to focus internally, remember the good breaks, and concentrate on the present.

Some tennis players get so wrapped up in their feelings and emotions that they fail to respond appropriately to the environmental factors influencing a match on a particular day. This is quite different from the self-focused tennis player who will typically benefit from being cool and collected. But sometimes such individuals become too involved with internal and self-related thoughts. These individuals have problems changing strategy when it would be beneficial. They tend to remain tied into a set strategy even when the situation demands that it be changed. Often such individuals are great students of the game who might make great teachers but think too much while performing. "Paralysis by analysis" can prevent a tennis player from being able to play up to her ability.

How about the tennis player with too broad an attentional style? This type of individual will have a tendency to have too

"Paralysis by analysis" can destroy your ability to execute skills.

many thoughts on her mind, with the result being an inability to consistently stick with one game plan or swing. Practice is often flighty and inconsistent. A player with this tendency may constantly shift from being an aggressive player to a conservative one without apparent reason. The player with a broad attentional tendency tends to be overanalytical and often will overreact to bad breaks or great play by the opposition. This type of tennis player may lose a match despite the best play of her life and decide to completely rebuild all her strokes, when such a change is not warranted.

A tennis player with a tendency for a narrow focus of attention will often spend most of her practice time on a few skills which may not be that crucial to success. For example, we all know individuals who spend all their practice time on the few shots at which they are already confident and skilled. The baseliner who practices only groundstrokes is a good example. Tennis players with this style do not analyze the full range of skills and strategies and therefore practice inefficiently. Such individuals may play well on certain days, on particular surfaces, or at a certain level of competition, but will be limited in their success because they are unwilling to direct their attention toward their weaknesses.

Try to be open and honest with yourself. What are your tendencies? Where might you change? Gather information from your friends, teacher, practice partners, and/or opponents. How would they describe your attentional style? Do they agree or disagree with your evaluations? If they disagree with your evaluation, don't decide that they are ignorant. Try to understand their reasoning. Do not allow yourself to argue with them. You asked for information. Take it and go home and analyze it. You decide if it can help you or not. Or if you do not wish to ask another player, take the following Attention-Distraction Inventory.

ATTENTION-DISTRACTION INVENTORY

Instructions: Circle the response which best describes your response to the situation described next to it. Answer each in terms of Strongly Agree, Mildly Agree, Mildly Disagree, Strongly Disagree.

Situation	*Strongly Agree*	*Mildly Agree*	*Mildly Disagree*	*Strongly Disagree*
1. If I make a mistake on a shot, I have difficulty putting it out of my mind while hitting my next shot.	4	3	2	1
2. When I serve I think about double-faulting.	4	3	2	1
3. I prepare to hit shots by carefully comparing my capabilities to the demands of the shot I'm about to try.	1	2	3	4
4. I wonder what others think about how I play.	4	3	2	1
5. I am self-conscious about my lack of power and I think about it when I'm hitting.	4	3	2	1
6. I am distracted by worries of missing backhands or overheads on important points.	4	3	2	1

Situation	*Strongly Agree*	*Mildly Agree*	*Mildly Disagree*	*Strongly Disagree*
7. When I play with others I get so involved with socializing and talking with them that I don't concentrate very well on my own game.	4	3	2	1
8. I always concentrate exclusively on the ball as I hit a shot.	1	2	3	4
9. I find myself thinking ahead to how I must do on the remaining points in order to win the game or set.	4	3	2	1
10. During a tournament I find myself overanalyzing my mistakes rather than thinking of hitting the shot I am about to hit perfectly.	4	3	2	1
11. I find that when I am playing tennis I think of other, unrelated things.	4	3	2	1
12. If I am about to hit a shot and someone on the next court talks, it distracts me and causes me to hit my shot poorly.	4	3	2	1
13. I always concentrate and use a preshot routine when I practice serving.	1	2	3	4
14. I find it difficult to vividly visualize the shot I am practicing.	4	3	2	1
15. I am so involved with understanding my weakest tennis strokes that I analyze them constantly while playing.	4	3	2	1

Scoring for Attention-Distraction Inventory: Add up the point values of the responses selected, and compare your score to the following scale.

Maximum Score = 60 My Total Score ________

Zone	*Score*	*Attention Control Level*
A	60–54	*Considerably below average:* great difficulty focusing your concentration
B	53–43	*Below average:* need to practice concentratating
C	42–30	*Average*
D	29–22	*Above average:* generally good at maintaining appropriate attention
E	21–15	*Considerably above average:* excellent attentional skills; seldom distracted

LEARNING TO CONTROL ATTENTION AND IMPROVE YOUR CONCENTRATION

All tennis players have particular strengths and weaknesses in their attentional control. Anyone wishing to master the game of tennis with its complex attentional demands must practice techniques designed to improve these abilities. Much like the physical side of tennis, you need to improve your attentional weaknesses and continue to maximize your strengths. For most tennis players, efforts should be spent in two main areas: (1) controlling the direction and width of attention and developing the ability to switch from one particular style to another (e.g., narrow-internal to broad-external) and (2) improving the length of time that you can maintain your concentration (attending to the immediate present rather than past or future thoughts). Both these attentional factors are greatly hindered by anxiety, and thus achievement-oriented tennis players must prepare themselves if they wish to effectively perform in stressful situations.

CONCENTRATION INPROVEMENT TECHNIQUES

• *Step 1.* Find a quiet room. Hold an action picture of one of your favorite tennis shots in front of you. Study the picture. Study the ball. If any distracting thoughts cross your mind, block them out. Repeat the word "ball" and get your mind back on the shot shown in the picture. Time how long you are able to maintain concentration the first few times you try this task. If a picture is not available or you would rather not use a picture, then go through the same process while imagining one of your favorite tennis shots.

Practice recognizing distracting thoughts as soon as they enter your mind and eliminate them by repeating the word "ball." Remember, it is seldom that anyone will play a tennis match without ever being distracted. The key is to not stay distracted for an extended period of time.

Each week record your longest concentration time for the week. Then chart your improvement while in a relaxed environment.

- *Step 2.* When you can maintain your concentration in step 1 for five minutes without being distracted, begin to practice in a distraction-filled environment (other people, TV or radio on, cars driving by, etc.). Again test your ability to concentrate at the start by timing yourself. When you can maintain concentration for five minutes in this environment, move on to step 3.
- *Step 3.* Practice maintaining your concentration while having some friends, family, or tennis partners attempt to distract you. Have them make personal statements about your physical appearance, your tennis strokes, your ability to perform under stress, or anything else which might make you feel self-conscious. Learn to deal with such statements at an intellectual rather than an emotional level. If you let them affect you emotionally, they can destroy your tennis game. When you can concentrate without being distracted in this situation for approximately three minutes, begin to practice controlling the width and direction of your attention.
- *Step 4.* Plan how you would like to play a particular point against an upcoming opponent. Decide how you would most ideally like to have the point played. Now close your eyes and totally concentrate on playing the point exactly as you had planned. When you are finished check your concentration. Were you distracted by another thought? Did you think of something else that you had to do? Did you question spending time on such a

boring task? If you did, you were distracted. Repeat the exercise over and over until you can play the point in your head without being distracted.

- *Step 5.* Repeat step 4, only this time do so with your eyes open. Concentrate totally on the point you wish to play. Let nothing distract you. If you do get distracted, immediately recognize it, "stop" the distracting thought, repeat "ball . . . ball . . . ," and concentrate again on the point.
- *Step 6.* Practice step 5 until you can repeat it five times without any distracting thoughts. When you can, try to concentrate on playing an entire game, and then a set, and then a match. Each time you do, practice recognizing distracting thoughts immediately when they occur and stopping them and redirecting attention so that you can concentrate.

These exercises will take time and effort. But if you do them regularly, your concentration will improve.

ATTENTIONAL PROBLEMS OF THE HIGHLY MOTIVATED

The tennis player who has a high level of achievement motivation and interest in improvement can sometimes be at a disadvantage in competition. High achievers sometimes realize on match or tournament day that they may not have mastered all aspects of their tennis game well enough to be winners in competition. This frequently brings forth a question from high achievers concerning their focus of attention. Such individuals understand that in practice a self-directed attentional focus will help them utilize proprioceptive information, or muscle and body sensations, to eliminate or at least improve on a detected flaw in their strokes. The high achiever realizes that to reach one's playing potential, each flaw needs to be eliminated. But the high-achieving tennis competitor also understands that focusing on improvement and centering attention internally on mechanics will not necessarily maximize his performance. The question often asked is, "Do I stop being concerned with improvement, and focus externally to maximize performance? Or do I concern myself with the future and continue to think, analyze, and learn throughout the tournament?"

Unfortunately, there is no easy solution to this dilemma because of a variety of related factors. A player who wishes to continue learning and practicing, has a self-focus, and may decide to "play through" a tournament. This choice may cause him to make some errors. A player who continues to analyze strokes during a tournament will be performing at a conscious rather than at a subconscious or automatic level. In other words, understand what you are doing. You have decided to prepare for the future. You have accepted the fact that your results might not be as good as possible. Remember this decision and don't let yourself become disappointed with performance errors and failure. Your performance will not be a true indication of your ability.

Certainly if you can't wait any longer and it definitely is time for you to compete, you must forget present improvement. Concentrate externally on the ball and let your strokes happen at a reflexive-automatic level. In other words, go play your best and be happy with it. Getting discouraged and thinking negatively hardly ever does anything helpful for your game.

4

Concentration = Control of Attention

The attentional control required of the tennis player is indeed challenging. It is not an easy task to concentrate throughout a match (one-and-one-half to three hours). Concentration may be especially trying when every shot you hit seems to be missing by an inch, and everything your opponent hits catches the line or hits the net cord and falls over for a winner.

For the competitive player there is no acceptable excuse for failure to concentrate. Once the competition starts no one cares that you might have been up late last night and are tired, or that you had a tough day at school, work, or home. Your opponent is not about to show sympathy. You alone are responsible for the challenge you have accepted. In tennis you have an activity in which the outcome is uncertain. It doesn't matter if you're playing someone that you think is worse than you, equal to you, or better than you. On any given day, depending to a great extent on your ability to concentrate, you can win or lose. If you are a highly competitive person who believes that winning is important to your identity, the challenge may be even greater. This may be especially true if you are competing against someone you love, dislike, or feel you should be better than. The knowledge that some people may give you status and friendship if you are a winner can make the task of controlling your attention during competition all the more difficult. Inappropriate and distracting thoughts related to any of these factors are likely to compete for your attention during competition. As we will discuss later, the more emotional involvement that you have the more difficulty you will have in controlling your attention.

The game of tennis places great demands on one's ability to control the width and direction of attention. Clearly, attention changes constantly while playing a tennis match. If you wish to be a consistent and effective tennis player, you must understand these attentional demands and learn how to control them.

Width of attention can be described on a continuum from a very narrow focus (one small thought or object) to a broad focus (many thoughts or objects). You may be aware that your mind frequently drifts along this continuum. But are you able to control it as you desire? Do you know where your attention should be along this dimension at differing times and situations in a tennis match?

Direction of attention can also be conceptualized as being on a continuum—from internally centered (inner thoughts and feelings about yourself) to externally centered (thinking of the ball, other people's thoughts or feelings, etc.). You are probably quite aware that your mind frequently drifts along these dimensions, but are you able to control it and shift it at will?

Let's look for a moment at attentional factors as they relate to a typical tennis match. Imagine that you are warming up for an important match against a new opponent. In this particular situation you initially need a *broad external* focus to gather all of the important information. Next, you must switch to a *broad internal* or self-focus to examine your own abilities and tendencies pertinent to how you are stroking the ball on this particular day. Once these decisions are made, the game strategy should be finalized. When it is time to play a point, you must now switch to a *narrow external* (ball) focus of attention. The information has been put into your "computer" and you must now visually focus on this one external thought. Your game plan, mental rehearsal, and physical practices should have programmed when you will hit the ball

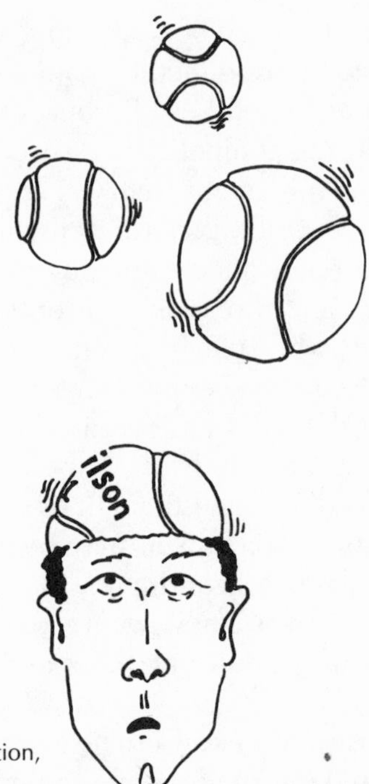

To improve your concentration, think only "ball."

(e.g., deep into a corner). When it is time to play a point, think only "ball." Simply respond to the ball and let the stroke be a reflexive response that the mind has programmed previously.

After execution of the shot, maintain the narrow external focus and observe the results. Shift to a narrow self-focus and capture the feeling of the shot. Finally, with a broad external focus, analyze the shot for correct and incorrect decisions and store it in the memory for future decisions through the use of a broad self-focus of attention.

Far too many tennis players get locked into a narrow self-focus (thinking body mechanics) during the stroke. This is most inappropriate if you wish to attain maximum performance. This internal attentional focus is most appropriate when you are learning tennis or are "working on your game" in practice. Your focus, however, must change to a narrow external focus on the ball when it is time to compete. It is most important to go through this thought process early in a match or for an entire set, especially if you are playing a new opponent. As the match progresses you should do less analysis between points or games (broad internal focus). By this point in a match you should have decided on a "game plan." Stay with that plan and concentrate on the ball. In a match against a well-known opponent you can get to this level of concentration right from the first point. Analysis should be done prior to the match or during warm-up.

Be sure you understand this important difference between attention in practice and performance. Prepare for competition by changing attention in practice to a more narrow external focus during the last days prior to the match.

The proprioceptive feedback gained from a narrow internal attentional style is most beneficial in learning "feel," but is most detrimental if you are thinking in this manner during play. If, on the other hand, you cannot focus internally or on your own feelings, you will not ever develop proper feel. If you cannot focus externally, you will not be able to visualize a successful shot. Constantly attempt to become aware of your strengths and weaknesses in this area. Strive to improve your weaknesses and maximize your strengths. Ultimately, you must be able to shift your attentional focus as required. Flexibility and adaptability in this area is crucial.

FOCUS OF ATTENTION FOR TENNIS

Warm-up:
- Broad external focus—gather all important information.
- Broad internal focus—self-focus on your own abilities.

Playing a Point:
- Broad external focus—decide where to hit the return.
- Narrow external focus—attend to ball only and execute the plan.

After the Shot is Executed:
- Narrow external focus—observe results of the shot.
- Narrow internal focus—capture the "feel" of the shot.
- Broad external focus—analyze the results for correct vs. incorrect planning.

CONCENTRATION AND ATTENTION IN TENNIS

It is obvious that anyone who desires to become a successful tennis player must first understand that concentration is as crucial, if not more crucial, than any of the mechanical skills which you may have been working on in practice. But simply knowing that concentration is important is not enough. You must also know what to focus your attention on during the course of a tennis match. Once this is understood you can begin mastering the skill of getting and keeping your attention where you direct it—*concentration.*

No one ever said that learning to concentrate during the pressure of a complex game like tennis was easy. It is in fact quite difficult. But keep in mind that it is a skill that is learned and can be greatly improved through understanding and practice. Because concentration and attention control will play such an important role in determining your future success or failure, you need to make sure that you give yourself time to understand and practice it.

In tennis each aspect of the game demands a very different attentional focus. Let's examine where your mind should be during the planning and execution of the different shots required in tennis.

THE SERVE

The serve is the stroke that you have complete control over. You and you alone *can* decide when, where, and how fast you will put the ball into play. It is most important that you benefit from the options and control presented to you when serving. To do otherwise is a waste of a most important weapon. To have put months and years of practice into the physical skill of serving and not be able to serve well when you need to is a waste of even more severe magnitude.

Many attentional changes take place while hitting the serve. Imagine that you are playing an opponent that you have never beaten before. You are serving at match point in the semifinals of a local tournament. In this situation you initially need a broad external focus before you serve so that you can bring together all the important information. Ask yourself which serve your opponent would rather return? Are more errors being produced on the backhand or forehand side? What will my opponent expect from me? If I hit to the backhand corner of the service box, where is the return likely to come?

Next, you, the server, must switch to a broad self-focus so that you can examine your abilities, consider how you have been hitting particular serves on this day, and compare them to the task demands (e.g., the specific situation and skills of your opponent). Once this information is analyzed and you have decided which shot to hit and where the return is likely to come, you must now switch to a series of narrow external and internal foci. The information has been analyzed. You must now preprogram your mind. You should visually imagine where your serve is going to land. Your narrow external thoughts allow you to rehearse the perfect execution of what is to come.

You must expect your serve to go in and you should expect the return. Next, you need to narrow your focus on yourself and feel the perfect shot that you have just imagined. Now, your *automatized* routine should occur (to be described later in this chapter). This routine should be very natural, and allowed to "just happen" as a result of systematic practice. Your last thoughts can then be narrow and external, with attention focusing totally on the ball. The body now simply has to carry out the plan it has been programmed to execute.

Although this process sounds fairly complex, it really isn't. It usually occurs in a matter of seconds.

There are many other situations that produce mental service errors. A typical one occurs when you start to worry about losing an important point and wasting a great opportunity. As the server you may start to take your time as you normally do, but suddenly fear that you are delaying too much and hit without ever getting your attention under control. The tendency to lose attentional control and flexibility in a stressful situation is well documented in sport psychology literature. If you allow this to happen, chances are that your mind will not be where it should be when you are serving. The result will be frequent errors that you need not make.

There is another different, but related, attentional mistake that tennis players often make. Far too many players get locked into a narrow self-focus (thinking body mechanics) during the stroke. This attentional focus may be appropriate when you are learning a shot or practicing to improve a mechanical weakness in a shot. But it is most inappropriate during competitive play.

Be sure that you understand this important difference between attention in practice and attention while performing. Prepare by practicing changes in attention in practice to a more narrowed external focus as you hit the ball, especially during the last days prior to competition. If your goal is to play to the best of your ability, it is time to forget about mechanical corrections. If you haven't got it mastered by now, forget about it until after the tournament. For the tournament have your last thoughts be of the ball (narrow external).

Your first thoughts upon preparing to serve in tennis should be to realistically compare your serving strengths and weaknesses to your opponent's returning strengths and weaknesses. If you do not know your opponent's game and did not learn anything about your opponent during warm-up, then make your decision based on your game alone.

Decide crucial strategies ahead of time. Will you begin the match by serving down the middle or wide? Will you go all-out on big points early in the match? When will you serve straight at the receiver and jam him? When will you hit offensively, and when will you play conservatively? When will you serve and volley, and when will you stay back? Many highly successful players prefer to program their first few service games ahead of time because they realize that they are likely to be somewhat nervous early in a match and make ineffective decisions.

Just as important as making these decisions is the need to anticipate where the individual receiving the serve is likely to return the ball. This decision is of course greatly influenced by whether or not you will come into net behind your serve. You must make this choice prior to actually serving the ball if you wish to maximize your effectiveness. This holds true for both your first and second serves.

Being realistic in making these strategy decisions is of great importance. Think it through ahead of time and in a rational manner, and stick with your choice unless momentum during the match dictates that you could or should do otherwise. One of the greatest errors a server can make is to serve and remain undecided as to whether or not she will come into the net or stay at the baseline. This is particularly likely to occur when you have double-faulted a few times or your opponent has hit some winning returns. However, the result of indecision is often to find yourself lost in thought and trapped a few feet inside the baseline. If you choose to serve and volley, believe in your ability to execute the manuever and come into net, and then do it. If you decide to stay back after you hit your serve, believe in your decision, get your feet behind the baseline at the appropriate angle for the return, and be ready to fight it out from there. Do not allow yourself to second-guess yourself once you have put the ball into play. If you are not comfortable with your decision, then don't put the ball into play until you are. Let nothing rush you.

A second attentional error that servers often make is to fail to expect the serve to come back. The cause of this problem may vary. The server may think that she has hit an ace and then stand there and applaud herself while the ball goes whizzing by. Or the server may expect to fault or double-fault and get lost in thoughts of self-pity or self-correction as the ball goes flying by. Either way, inappropriate attentional factors have prevented you from utilizing your skills in a most productive manner.

SEQUENCE OF ATTENTION FOR A GOOD TENNIS SERVE*

1. Broad external focus—to gather the information needed to assess the requirements of the serve and examine the personal abilities and preferences of your opponent.
2. Broad self-focus—examine your personal abilities and preferences.
3. Narrow external focus—select the specific serve and concentrate on the target (where to hit the serve).
4. Narrow self-focus—feel the perfect serve.
5. Narrow external focus—think target and focus on goal.
6. Shot runs off automatically—think ball.

*You must practice this sequence until it is automatic. It should be an automatic rather than a conscious process when you compete.

Establish a Service Routine and a Rhythm

Anyone who wants to develop effective first and second serves that will hold up under the stress of competitive pressure must develop a routine. With consistent practice, a routine for your serve will become habitual and automatic. It will become a natural part of your serve. It will give you a rhythm and a sense of comfort that will not escape you on your first or second serve no matter how tension-filled the situation. Watch Martina Navratilova, Jimmy Connors, Tracy Austin, John McEnroe, or Roscoe Tanner the next time you have the opportunity. You will notice that their routines and the timing of their routines remain the same throughout a match. This is no accident. It has been planned, practiced, and perfected so that it will help them feel comfortable and force them to take their time during competition.

For most players a routine should begin by placing the toe of the forward foot (left for a right-hander or right for a left-hander) a set distance behind the baseline. The distance behind the line is not so important as keeping the distance consistent. As you prepare to serve, be consistent in placing both feet the same distance from the baseline and the same distance apart each time. Be certain that you are well-balanced.

Next, set your grip in your hand and place the ball or balls in your tossing hand. It should be pointed out that there are some distinct benefits to always serving (in practice and in competition) with only one ball in your hand. First, all you have to learn is one toss. If you hold two balls when you get ready for your first serve and one ball for your second serve, you must master two different tosses. Second, by using one ball in your hand and one in your pocket you will be forced to slow down and take your time and go through the exact *same* routine for each and every serve. For many players there is a self-defeating tendency to rush through their second serve. Unfortunately, for some, the more important the point, the quicker they put the second serve in play. Better players use their routine to help them take the same amount of time on all important points. The next time you play, check yourself. Do you rush your second serve so that you can get it over with quickly, or do you remain calm, keep with your routine, and take your time?

If part of what we have been discussing appears trivial to you, you may need to reappraise your thinking to understand its importance. People who want to improve and get the most out of their abilities recognize first of all that these seemingly minor points are indeed crucial. Secondly, they realize that they are part of the differences between a consistent server and one that is "on" one day and "off" the next. Thirdly, they know that they must discipline themselves to decide on the type and placement of the serve and visually imagine its perfect execution prior to each serve.

The next step in your routine should be to take a very deep, slow breath and let go of the tension in your body, particularly in your fingers, wrists, arms, shoulders, and upper back. Now visualize in your mind the exact area where you want your serve to land. As you gain in experience you will gain a court sense and be able to do this without even looking at the court. Now "feel" the exact serve that you will hit. If your opponent makes a quick move to distract you or anything else happens that breaks your concentration, stop and start over again. With practice you will learn to immerse yourself in *your* routine so that nothing will interfere with your attention.

Next, select a particular number of times to bounce the ball with your tossing hand before you actually toss the ball for your serve. It does not matter if you bounce the ball two, three, or five times. Be comfortable with that number of bounces and practice it daily. If at any time something happens that breaks up the rhythm of your ball bounces, stop, catch the ball, get in balance, and start over again. Once again, do not let anyone or anything prevent you from going through your routine in the precise manner that you have practiced it. Remember, you and you alone are in control of the serve.

All that now remains is for you to toss and hit the serve. When you toss the ball, you will find it most helpful to pick a spot (generally above and in front of you) where you want the toss to end. Focus your attention on this spot and direct your toss to this spot. Now simply let go and focus all your attention on the ball. Hit it to your preselected target. Be sure that you do not aim or push the ball—let your serve run off as you had planned.

Remember, you must practice this routine on a regular basis until it is automatic and habitual. You will know you have accomplished this goal when you find yourself consistently using your routine on all your serves—even important serves in big matches. As you go through the process of mastery of your routine, be certain that you continue to learn, grow, and understand events, situations, and opponents that distract you or make you tense and therefore cause you to serve ineffectively. The better you can understand yourself, the better you will be able to anticipate situations that are likely to hurt your performance. Eventually, it will not matter whether the sun is in your eyes, there is strong wind, it is a match point, or an opponent is hitting great returns. You will be able to concentrate on what you want to do, stick with your routine, and perform up to your *true* potential. With time, understanding, and experience, you will realize that you should take more time on your serves on important points. You will find that sometimes you will still think, "I sure hope I don't double-fault and lose this point and game." The difference will be that you will recognize this inappropriate thought and stop for a moment to get your body comfortable and your mind thinking in an effective manner before you start your routine again.

Don't forget that seemingly anxious thoughts on match point, such as "I better not get this serve near her forehand because she has been crunching them all day," can be very important and helpful. The key is to read this thought in an intellectual manner. Decide what this information means in terms of where you should hit your serve, plan your serve, get into your routine, and then make your plan happen.

As you gain in confidence and you ingrain these strategies, keep in mind that you may still sometimes fail to control your mind to the desired degree. Rather than getting frustrated and causing further serving problems, recognize your mistakes and try to understand your errors. Use the information gained to anticipate when you might lose your concentration in the future.

This approach will help you to gradually reduce the frequency of mental errors that you make and hasten the quickness with which you regain mental control following the errors.

SERVICE ROUTINE

1. Hold only one ball in hand, second ball in pocket.
2. Set foot position and attain balance.
3. Adjust racket grip and ball.
4. Decide on service style and directional placement.
5. Visually imagine effective serve.
6. Bounce ball a set number of times if part of your individualized routine, and breathe deeply.
7. Focus attention on tossing ball to a spot (generally above and in front of body) where you want the toss to end.
8. Watch ball and serve to programmed spot.

Service Return Strategy

As you await an oncoming serve, all the pressure is on you. You must watch the ball leave the server's racket. You must simultaneously be aware of subtle changes in racket position, react to the speed and spin of the serve, and then execute the stroke which will place the ball in the desired place on the opponent's court. If all these decisions were left to the last minute, the task would be overwhelming.

A preplanned strategy for returning the serve would be one way to reduce the decision-making demands. If you already know where you wish to return the serve, you can focus almost exclusively on the task at hand. Determining a service return strategy should include (1) where to stand in order to cover your opponent's serving possibilities, (2) where to aim the ball, and (3) how to stroke it (chip, topspin, etc.).

The return of serve is a shot that challenges the minds of even the best players. It is a shot that often separates the best from the rest. The opportunity for "failures of the mind" to destroy a normally smooth and precise stroke is everpresent. Only players who have mastered the ability to "clear the mind" and concentrate on the task at hand are able to master this aspect of the game of tennis.

Certainly mastery of the return of serve does not suggest that you will be free of occasional ineffective returns or "bad" games. You may even struggle for an entire set or match. Mastery of the return of serve means that others will have to serve very well to beat you. You will not beat yourself. You will regularly and aggressively hit the return where you want to hit it in any situation.

Many players fail to be successful at returning serve because they allow themselves to become intimidated, uptight, and mentally distracted. The result can be a stroke that is much quicker than normal, or one with a finish that is much shorter than normal with the weight falling backward rather than forward. Often the receiver appears to be uptight and off-balance. Some players become so distracted that they even forget to watch the ball.

Chances are that you are well aware of these problems and a host of others. You are probably also aware of the fact that many different factors can cause you to respond in this manner. A big, tall server who intimidates you, a slow, low-spinning slice serve that causes you to overhit, a high, bouncing kick serve, a serve that jams your body, or a server who hits the lines on the court from all angles—any of these can destroy your return of serve. You possibly have experienced all or some of these situations.

Rather than dwell on each of these problems, you must develop a solution to all of them: a solution that will help you learn how to return serve effectively when faced with pressure-filled situations.

To help you understand how important your thinking is to your return of serve, think for a moment of your return of serve in doubles. Often players do much better at returning serve in doubles than in singles because they are forced to make a conscious decision ahead of time as to where they will hit the ball. It is amazing how accurately and consistently you can return serve when you preprogram your mind and body correctly. Frequently, you may be mentally lazy in singles and not even decide where you wish to return the ball.

How often in the past have you found that your return of serve in singles gets much better when a baseliner starts coming to net behind serve? Unless you are intimidated by a net rusher, this situation forces you to concentrate more on your return. It forces you to make a decision on where to hit your return.

Of course, it is also possible that your return of serve *really* falls apart when you are faced with either of the situations just described. If this is true for you, your problem isn't one of mental laziness. Most likely you are somewhat anxious and distracted by the worry that you will miss your return. Either way, your mind and attention is not focused where it should be, and you will benefit from thinking in the manner suggested below.

An effective return of serve begins with your preshot preparation. Before every return, you must plan your strategy. You must learn to step up to receive a serve only after you have decided for *certain* where you will hit your return. If you are uncertain, there will be doubt in your mind and you will be in trouble. Discipline yourself to decide ahead of time whether you will return serve down the line, cross-court, or down the center of the court. You must also determine whether you will lob, chip and come in, or drive the ball with topspin. Nothing could be worse than to be in the middle of deciding whether to chip and come in or drive the ball halfway through the server's motion when it's time to hit. Chances are that such a confused state will result in an unsuccessful return. So if you haven't decided for sure *where* and *how* to hit your return, turn away from the server *until you are ready.*

Once you have decided where and how to hit your return, you should be thinking and saying "ball" or some other, similar cue phrase to yourself. Concentrate on watching only the ball in the server's hand. Follow it all the way through the server's motion. Do not let anything else enter your mind or your field of vision. You will automatically hit the ball where you have already programmed your body to hit it. Let it happen.

Forget about trying to read the server's toss or service

motion. You are much better off focusing on the ball and reacting to it. At the advanced levels of tennis about half the cues that you are trying to read will be deceptive moves designed to fool you.

The only time that it might be to your advantage to interpret cues would be against an opponent who is consistently hitting both the center line and the sideline short and wide. On such days, your only hope may be to go ahead and guess. Possibly you can unnerve the server and get a few service breaks.

There is no magic that makes these mental strategies work. You need to correctly tell your body what to do if you wish it to perform effectively. Likewise, if you are telling your body what to do, your mind *can't be thinking about what could go wrong, what you might have done* (second-guessing yourself), or *worrying about what might result.* In addition, there are positive, productive thoughts which will help you remain calm and in control of your emotions.

With time and practice you will find that your return of serve will get both more consistent and more aggressive. You will most likely also find out that at times your return will get really grooved and you will start hitting great returns all over the court. Through some combination of your confidence and your opponent's lack of confidence resulting from your superior returns you will find that sometimes during a match you will not have to program your returns and consciously think of the ball. For some not completely understood reason you will be able to feel the right shot and concentrate without trying at all. Your body just seems to know where to hit the ball and it happens. Do not feel that you should fight this experience. Enjoy it and let it happen. But stay alert. If you start missing or if your opponent gets hot, get your attention back to where we suggested it should be. If you are not mentally attentive, you can get lackadaisical, lose your confidence, get anxious, and allow the momentum to turn in your opponent's favor.

This positive, productive attitude toward your mental approach will also help you in concentrating on game, set, or match points. These are situations where you may begin anticipating winning or losing—distracting and inappropriate thoughts for maximizing your performance.

ROUTINE FOR RECEIVING SERVE

1. Relax and take deep breaths as you take your ready position.
2. Look at opponent in relation to the court.
3. Decide on where you will return the shot.
4. Stand in ready position and picture your return, including the flight of the ball.
5. Feel the shot with your whole body. (If it does not feel good, STOP—and start over again. Do not get lazy or self-conscious and simply allow the server to hit. Most likely if you do, it will not result in a good return.)
6. Think ball and respond to it.

Important points also cause many players to alter their strokes. Some players tend to hit the return less aggressively and others tend to get overly aggressive and go for too many perfect winners. Unfortunately, many people have learned, while at the lower levels of play, that "pushing" the ball back can be quite successful. Often at this level the other player will make a mistake and give you the point, but as you advance such a strategy is no longer effective. At the advanced levels of play better players still give themselves room for error on the sidelines but they hit out on their returns and go for depth. On returning second serves in particular, top players will move in and try to get to the net first and put the pressure on the opponent. If you wish to do this, it is particularly important that you take your time. Do not step up to return on "big points" until you have decided what you are going to do with your return. You must decide and believe in your decision if you wish to execute it effectively. You will find that this same aggressive and confident service return strategy will work for you at the start of a match. If you think correctly, you may often get an early service break. If not, you will at least be hitting out and getting used to hitting out on your opponent's serve so that you will be able to get a break soon. This approach to returning also has a tendency to keep your opponent from feeling comfortable. Even if you're missing and hitting the top of the net or just missing lines, your opponent is forced to recognize that you are not intimidated. You are a confident and aggressive player who will be tough to beat.

Prior to your match you may even wish to decide that once every so many games you will hit a soft, low return of service. This is especially true against a serve-and-volley player. The more aggressive your normal service return becomes, the more effective an occasional soft, low return will be. If you wish to use this shot, you must believe in it. Convince yourself it will work before you try it, and be ready to move in behind it and attack if the opponent hits you back a short ball. To hit a perfect soft, short return and then get caught standing at baseline wondering if it will clear the net or if the opponent will get it is a mistake you don't want to make. Usually getting caught flatfooted and watching is a result of failing to *expect that your shot will be good* or that your opponent will return it. You must always expect your shots to be good—and that your opponent will return them.

A couple of final points regarding your service return. First, if you're in a match that you wish to win, do not decide to try to hit a return that is not in your repertoire. Save those dreams for practice. You will probably not be confident enough to execute the planned shot. Second, realize that no matter how well you have planned, some serves will fool you. Sometimes you *will make errors.* Even the best do. Other times, you will be jammed so tight, or extended so far, that you may have to hit the ball whenever or however you can. Your success on these shots will be determined by a combination of your experience and your natural instincts.

THE APPROACH SHOT

The approach shot, which to the unknowing observer appears to be the simplest of shots, can at times be the most frustrating of shots. A few missed opportunities can do terrible things to the minds of mere mortals. Fortunately, most of the problems with this shot, once you have developed the required strokes, are caused by the mind. Clearly, the easier a shot appears to be, the more frustration it can cause when it is missed. Frustration often leads to a distracted and uncontrolled mental state.

One key to hitting consistent approach shots is to stroke the ball smoothly and deep and be sure not to overhit the shot. Keep this thought in mind as we explain an effective mental strategy for the approach shot and how failure to use such an approach often leads to overhitting and frequent errors (and occasionally a winner).

Prior to any game, set, or match you must plan your mental strategy for your approach shots. Where and how you will hit these shots must be decided ahead of time. You cannot allow yourself to haphazardly go into a match and make decisions as you are about to hit your approach shot. Make your decision ahead of time. Stick with your choice and watch the ball.

A player could do quite well in tennis if she decided to hit every approach shot deep and down the line. Doing so allows you to concentrate only on the ball, which will greatly benefit your consistency on this shot. But if you wish to rise to the top in tennis, you must learn to vary your approach shots. You must be able to hit cross-court, down the line, down the center, deep, short and wide, and even a variety of drop shots off the short ball. Unfortunately, the more options that you give yourself, the more likely you are to become mentally confused and distracted. The result may be indecision, failure to think and watch the ball, and frequent errors. But without a doubt, there are also great advantages to variation. Most important, your opponent will constantly be off guard and unsure of where your approach shot will be hit. You will soon find that effective execution of this strategy will allow you the luxury of not needing to hit your approach shots so hard.

In order to execute this strategy and maintain your concentration on the ball you must decide ahead of time where and how you will hit your next approach. Do not change your mind when the next short ball comes, no matter what your opponent does. Forget about all the feigning and scrambling that your opponent is doing at the baseline. None of it matters. *You must know where you are going to hit the ball.* So concentrate on watching the ball and hit it where you planned on hitting it no matter where your opponent is. Your approach shots will become more consistent. Your opponent won't know where your shots are going and your opponent will have to beat you. You will not beat yourself. So decide on your strategy, and when approach shots occur stick with your decision; think "ball" and be prepared for your next shot.

THE VOLLEY

Despite the fact that the volley may be the simplest shot to execute, many players fail to learn to hit it. Most fail because they are afraid to come near the net. Most who have this problem fear that they will get hurt by the ball; others fear that they will get lobbed and not be able to cover it.

Both these fears can lead to greater problems which are sure to affect the successful development of your game. If your fear prevents you from coming to net you will probably never develop an approach shot or an overhead. If you do manage to develop them, you will most likely never get to use them in a match. If your main problem is the fear of getting lobbed (or passed), the solution is fairly specific. Practice going back to hit overheads until you have it mastered, and do quickness drills at the net. Getting your body into great condition will also help.

The person who avoids the net completely or who comes to net but consistently misses is an entirely different story. If this is your problem you must first of all recognize that most players are somewhat anxious when they first get near the net. You must also realize that your anxious thoughts are going to distract you, cause you to get uptight, and increase the likelihood that you will get hit or volley poorly. Either of these reactions is likely to cause you to feel even more uncomfortable about getting to the net.

Think back for a moment to what was said earlier about assessing your thoughts prior to, during, and following attempts to go to net to volley. Do you tend to fear getting hit or embarrassing yourself? What do you think about as the ball is coming to you? After trying to hit a volley how do you feel and think?

In our work with players who are afraid of the net, we often find that even the mention of the word "volley" conjures up anxiety-inducing negative feelings and thoughts. To overcome this problem, you must begin by recognizing that coming to the net really isn't very dangerous. If you're worried about getting passed or lobbed, forget it. Even the best pros have this happen to them. The key is to start perceiving the situation differently. Look at it like this. The more frequently you come to net, the more you will put the pressure on your opponent. Thus, your opposition is more likely to make a mistake and give you a point than she is likely to pass you. So start noticing how often you force an error or set yourself up for a point, relative to how often you get passed. If you frequently set yourself up, but miss the volley, start enjoying these misses. The more you get into this situation, the faster your volley and your game will improve. With time, your misses at the net will become winners. Be sure to think about the future even if it's a year or two away. In a year you will thank yourself. Besides helping your volley, this effort will help your approach shots, your overheads, your half-volley, and even your footwork as you are forced to move in all directions.

But what do you do if your problem is fear of the ball? A good idea is to recognize that inappropriate thoughts are likely to cause you to get hit and add to your problems. When you are at the net you should be thinking "step to ball." If you find that your thoughts are something quite different, get in the habit of verbalizing "step to ball" each time that you attempt a volley. Don't think that this is the entire solution. You must gradually expose yourself to volleying until you feel comfortable at net and then develop the shot through hours of practice.

For most players who are even slightly afraid of being hit, the traditional approach of having someone hit bullets to you at the net until you are used to it will not work. It will just convince you all the more that you want nothing to do with coming to net. Get a friend that you trust to *throw* balls *slowly* to *either side* of your body while you stand at net and volley while saying "step to ball" either out loud or to yourself. As you gain in confidence have your partner *throw* the balls, again *slowly*, right at your body. Once again think "step to ball" as you volley. Very gradually increase the speed at which the balls are thrown. When you feel that you are ready (not when your friend thinks you're ready) have the balls *hit* to you with a racket. Once again start out slowly and gradually increase the speed. Remember to keep repeating "step to ball" and block out any other thoughts. With time and instruction on mechanics you will develop an effective volley.

THE HALF-VOLLEY

If you can hit a volley, you can hit a half-volley. But you must not let the shot intimidate you. Certainly you must get the mechanics down first, but most people miss this shot because they let the ball control them. They fall backward and hit the ball late. So bend down, shift your weight forward, and soon you will have it.

In general, the remaining shots required for success in tennis demand that you focus all your attention on one simple thought—"ball." It doesn't really matter if you are in the middle of an extended rally from the baseline or hitting a passing shot at match point. You must decide where to hit the shot, believe in your decision, and watch the ball.

THE OVERHEAD

The overhead is possibly the most enjoyable and intimidating of shots. It is a shot well worth mastering. It will give your game an exciting new dimension.

To consistently hit an overhead you must quite simply watch the "ball" and "go get it." Nothing should distract you from your concentration. Most players can lose concentration in several different situations. Playing someone who anticipates well and is quick can cause even an advanced player to start trying to sneak a look at the opponent or to try to overhit the overhead. Against such a player it is crucial to decide on a strategy. Will you hit the open court or will you hit behind the speedy baseliner? Make your decision and then stick with it. The only time that it is acceptable to look at the opponent is if you get a short lob that you can let bounce before you smash it. But even in this case your attention must be back on the ball by the time it bounces. Your mind must be totally focused on the ball.

The second situation that often distracts is when you have missed two or three overheads in a row. It is easy to start thinking about body mechanics or body position when this occurs. You will have to work to control your mind and attend to the ball. A very effective way to concentrate is to simply repeat the word "ball" over and over so you don't allow your mind to think of all the other things that can distract you.

The third situation that you must be prepared for is playing in rough weather. This may include particularly windy or bright, sunshiny days. The first key is to make sure you practice as much as possible under these conditions. It will help you begin to feel comfortable with the conditions. Too many players dislike these conditions, so they fail to ever practice in them and thus never learn to play well in them. If you will practice in them, two very positive things will happen: (1) you will find out that you can hit overheads in these conditions, and (2) you will begin to love competing in these conditions because you will know that the worse the conditions, the more the advantage you will have.

Once you have concentrated and watched the ball, you must make sure that you expect your overhead to be good, yet always move in and expect it to come back. Do not get caught standing and taking a picture of a great shot. It may not come back, but always be prepared in case it does. By doing so, you will be ingraining a good habit so that when you play someone who does hit it back you will be ready and in position.

Much of what we have said about the overhead is also true for the drop shot, lob, and groundstroke—you must accept your decisions and believe your shots will be successful. Get totally absorbed in the ball. If you are going to hit a drop shot, focus on the ball *and* expect it to go over the net *and* expect your opponent to get it back. Move in after you hit it, think ball, and put it away. Do not hit a drop shot and get caught standing and wondering if it will go in or if your opponent will get to it. A mental approach such as this will only paralyze your feet and lose points.

The same principle applies to hitting a lob. Regardless of whether you are hitting an offensive or defensive lob, make your decision, believe it is the right decision, watch the ball, and hit it. Then, if it's a defensive lob, designed to get you back into position on a point, move your feet and expect the ball to come back and expect to return it. Again, concentrate on the ball. If you're hitting an offensive topspin lob be sure you think ball and finish your shot. Again, always expect that your shot will be in the court and be ready to attack.

COMPETITIVE DISTRACTORS

There are many situations that occur during the course of play that demand special attention. It is quite easy to lose control of the width and direction of your attention in any of these situations. You must learn to anticipate them, realize how you might be distracted, and understand how to keep your attention focused properly.

Playing in Front of Friends

Almost anyone can concentrate if they are playing in the middle of the woods on a remote court. There are no distractions other than your opponent. But take that same court, the same opponent, and add even five people whom you care about as an audience and you have an entirely new situation. The potential for distraction may be amplified if you want to impress your friends. It is quite easy to have your concentration drift to an external direction and focus on the audience or to focus internally on your own thoughts. Perhaps you are thinking about how badly you are embarrassing yourself. Or you may also be thinking about how much you are impressing them. Either way, you are distracted. You are either playing poorly or you are about to start playing poorly if you keep thinking about how well you are doing.

The moment you recognize that you are distracted, shift to a narrow external focus and think "ball"; for a short time keep checking your attention in between points until you naturally get absorbed into the play.

Coping with Pace

Does a real big hitter or a real soft hitter destroy your game? How do players with either of these types of playing styles affect your concentration? Do you still think "ball" or do you get distracted? Either a fast or slow pace can affect your thinking and therefore your footwork and the smoothness and rhythm of your swing. Often the result is a quick, jerky stroke.

The next time you come up against a big hitter, relax and think rationally for a moment. If the ball is hit faster to you, half your work is already done. You will be able to hit it back as hard as usual with much less effort and a much shorter backswing. So let your opponent do the work and use his or her speed to *your* advantage. Stay under control and think "ball."

Often just the opposite effect occurs when you play someone who gives you no pace. You worry that you can't ever put the ball away so you start overhitting and missing everywhere. You must realize that a player with no pace cannot hurt you unless you let her get into your head. So decide before the match ever starts how you will play. If you decide to be patient, get ready to stay on the court all day if necessary. Often this alone will upset your opponent's game. If this is your game plan, you must stay with it without questioning or second-guessing yourself. On the other hand, if you decide that you must attack this player in order to win, accept your decision and attack. Stay calm if you miss a lot of shots early. It may take some time to get your timing down against the slow pace. Just keep telling yourself to think "ball" because with time your shots will start going in and you will take control of the match. Do not ever doubt that this will happen. If you do, you will most likely get lost in your thoughts and never know what you want to do, let alone watch the ball.

PLAYING A STEADY BASELINE BLOOPER

Undoubtedly there are players who typically lose extended baseline rallies because they lose their patience and attention and hit a poor shot. But losing your patience begins as a result of not anticipating ahead of time that there will be many extended cross-court rallies. If you wish to be successful against a baseliner with patience, you must decide ahead of time how you are going to play the person. How long will you stay at the baseline? When will you attack? Can you attack off either side? Will you only attack on short balls? Will you hit drop shots to draw the player to the net? If you do, what will you do next?

There is no way that you can concentrate on the ball if you don't know what shot to hit next. This is especially true when you are playing an opponent who is better than you or your equal. If you are constantly making decisions and then second-guessing yourself, chances are good that you will be confused and hit a "dumb" shot. This confused mental state explains the drop shot hit at match point by the player who never uses or practices a drop shot. An unforced error is the usual result. So once again we emphasize the importance of anticipating game situations, making realistic decisions, believing in them, and then focusing on the ball and letting it happen. Remember, the main reason that the unforced error occurs is due to confusion and self-doubt which prevent you from thinking "ball."

A baseline blooper utilizes the strategy of distracting your attention by outsteadying you—"driving you nuts." You must, therefore, have the right frame of mind, be willing to be patient, and eventually outfox your opponent in an aggressive fashion. Baseliners are very consistent players, and they count on your falling into their game plan. This is no problem if you are more consistent from the baseline than the opponent. But if you are not, you need alternate plans. To combat a baseliner, you must maintain your concentration and constantly look for an opening in which you can take the initiative. Be alert for a chance to force the play or bring your opponent to the net. The key to success is to move the ball around, from side to side and with varied trajectory and pace. Try to avoid hitting shots that will let the baseliner get into a rhythm.

If you wish to practice your baseline concentration, try a game of "B and B" (baseline-to-baseline). In this practice, you rally with your practice partner from baseline to baseline, counting the number of times your shots land between the service line and the baseline. If you hit a short ball, stop the count (or award your opponent a point) and begin again. This practice will help you develop the patience necessary to combat a "baseliner."

Most baseliners attempt to lull you to sleep with high, bouncing balls. To counteract these, learn to take the ball on the rise by hitting the ball at waist level as it comes up off the court. This requires good preparation with the racket back, ready to hit the ball on the rise.

Tennis demands both short-term and long-term concentration. In particular, many players have difficulty maintaining their attention during long points. One way to learn to deal with the demands of long points is to play long points during practice by keeping the rally going as long as possible. This is not always possible for less skilled players, but they can utilize techniques such as holding extra balls to be put into play immediately after a miss, or playing "out balls" on the bounce to force longer periods of concentration.

You may also wish to practice in distracting circumstances. Schedule some practice at a noisy local court, or play near traffic or in stiff winds. After such practice, you should learn to cope with the distractions and be able to handle them when they are most important—during a match.

Concentration is also essential if you hope to take advantage of the net. This can happen in either of two ways: (1) bringing the opponent to the net or (2) attacking the net yourself. In the first option, the baseliner is forced to come to the net, where he is at a disadvantage. At that point you should be able to win the point with a passing shot, or take over the offense with a well-placed lob. In the second option, you should elect to "jump all over" a short shot from your opponent so that you gain the offensive and place pressure on your opponent.

CONTROLLING MOMENTUM

Players who are winners know how to take control of a match. Sometimes they take charge from the very beginning and sometimes they start out slowly. But when they need to, winners swing the momentum in their direction. At the professional level all players have highly developed physical skills. But only the very best are able to completely believe in themselves and concentrate on attacking the ball and hitting it deep on important points.

Everyone who plays recognizes when a big point is about to present itself. Many unsuccessful players get lost thinking about how crucial the point will be and get lost in thoughts related to its importance. Better players recognize the importance of the point, *look forward* to playing it, decide how to play it (usually aggressively), and then concentrate completely on the ball. Nothing should enter the mind. Thoughts of missing or losing the point are completely blocked out. The winner recognizes that they are completely irrelevant to the task at hand. But sometimes players of this caliber also lose their concentration and make mistakes. Don't think for a moment that they don't. A major difference is that when they make a mistake they recognize it and recover much more readily than the average player.

It is particularly interesting to note that players who "know how to win" not only play more aggressively when they are ahead or playing well, but when they are behind as well.

Keep in mind that playing aggressively doesn't mean that you must come into net. It may simply mean a little more pace, a little more depth, a little closer to the lines. Anything that puts the pressure on the opposition will suffice. Your shots should be intentionally planned for that purpose. You know that they will work.

Depending on the level of your game, this may or may not be the best plan for you on "big" points. If you are not an advanced player, you may be better off playing more cautiously and giving yourself more room for errors. Whatever your decision strategically, make it ahead of time and then stay with it.

Anytime you are playing an important game or point (perhaps serving for the match), you must strive to concentrate totally in the present. You must play one point at a time. For many the tendency is to get distracted by thinking of the future, about winning or losing. Thoughts related to how great you will feel when you win or how badly you will feel if you lose are distracting. They are therefore self-defeating. Recognize such thoughts, stop them, and lock into the present.

PLAYING WITH PAIN OR WHEN TIRED

Anyone who plays competitive tennis sooner or later experiences pain during competition. The pain may be caused by either injury or tiredness.

If you are injured, the first step is to evaluate your injury. How serious is the injury? Will it hurt to continue playing? Is it worth it to continue playing?

Once you have decided to continue, you must be capable of blocking out any thoughts related to the pain. If you can't, you will probably be distracted and play poorly.

Realize that most people who compete at tennis will only feel tired or hurt when they are losing or playing poorly. The mind has a curious habit of looking for an excuse or an escape. You must be careful to not fall prey to a psychological escape. Do not allow yourself to develop the excuse of faking injury or believing that you are too tired to continue. If you do not fight it, the mind will allow you to continue. It is your job to learn to differentiate between real and imagined injury or tiredness. When you decide that it is imagined, focus your attention on the ball and play.

5
Anxiety and Performance

When you start to worry about possible negative results, your anxiety can have a detrimental effect on your tennis game. Psychologically, when you become fearful of losing, making a mistake, hitting into the net, or double-faulting, you diminish your ability to control your attention.

It does not matter whether your reasons for becoming anxious are real (I can't hit a backhand) or imagined (I don't think I can hit a backhand). Your body will still go into a state of preparedness for danger known as "fight-or-flight" syndrome. Have you ever awakened in the middle of the night in a cold sweat from a bad dream? Have you ever walked down a dark street in a strange city late at night and heard a sudden noise? It does not matter that there was no real danger. Just the thought of danger can initiate the fight-or-flight response with real bodily reactions. The fight-or-flight syndrome is an automatic response mechanism designed to help you in dangerous situations. It is a marked hindrance to you when you are attempting to concentrate and execute effective tennis strokes.

When you become anxious about a particular stroke, even if for no apparent reason, a signal is sent to the hypothalamus which releases a hormone that triggers the nearby pituitary gland. The pituitary sends a hormone (ACTH) which tells the adrenal glands to release several hormones, including adrenaline, norepinephrine, and cortisone. These hormones are designed to prepare your mind and body for an emergency situation. Your heartbeat and breathing speed up, and panting allows you to quickly eliminate carbon dioxide. The muscles of your body in general begin to tighten. You no longer accurately differentiate between muscles that should be relaxed or tensed. Even the muscles surrounding your lungs and bronchial tubes tend to tighten, with resulting shortness and shallowness of breath (and eventually the sensation of "choking"). To make up for this shortness of breath, breathing becomes more rapid.

If the situation were severe enough, you would actually "choke" to death. Such is often the case with many individuals who have supposedly drowned, but have no water in their lungs. The anxious thoughts you perceive while playing tennis may indeed cause you to experience some choking sensation. Your heartbeat may speed up, with rapid breathing and increased sweating. You may feel tired due to excess tension and excess carbon dioxide. You may experience a loss of control of your attention and a tendency to make "dumb" decisions. (Have you ever needed one more point to finish a set or beat a player you have never before defeated, and found yourself trying a shot you have never before attempted, let alone successfully executed? Have you ever completely changed your playing style, or hit before you had made up your mind, because your mind was moving too quickly?)

You may also be aware that when you are highly anxious your digestive system shuts down, the esophagus contracts, and the gastric juices stop flowing. This can make you feel nauseous, and is a good reason why you may not want to play a big match on a full stomach. In order to maximize the efficient use of your larger muscle groups, blood vessels near the surface of the skin as well as in the hands and feet close down and divert their blood supply to the larger, deeper muscles. Thus, you can understand the sensation of cold hands or feet when you're nervous and why a "touch" or "fine feel" skill like serving or hitting drop shots may be so greatly affected by anxiety.

Many tennis players, especially the great ones like Andrea

Jaeger or Bjorn Borg, have used this syndrome to their advantage. They have called on that flow of adrenaline at a crucial time to hit the ball just a little bit firmer. For them, *when they are playing well and are confident,* it works and is helpful. But even for them, if they are in a slump and have lost their confidence, the extra adrenaline can cause them to try too hard and overhit. Thus, an important distinction must be made. It is one thing for a self-confident, successful tennis player who has been slightly bored and underaroused to try to "psych up" at crucial times to maximize performance. It is quite another thing for a player who lacks self-confidence, or even for the same skillful player when not playing well and low on self-confidence, to attempt to psych down, to lower their anxiety or arousal level.

It is well documented that there is an "inverted-U" relationship between an individual's level of arousal and his performance. In other words, for each tennis player there is a moderate level of arousal at which tennis performance will peak (see Figure 1). If you are above or below this level your performance will deteriorate. Most tennis players have a problem being overaroused, and thus most of the techniques in this book are designed to control overarousal and anxiety-related problems. Of course, if you are bored with a match or your opponent, or just plain "tennised out," your problem is underarousal; relaxing more would certainly not be beneficial to your game. It is at times like these that it may indeed be a good idea to start talking to yourself, even negatively, to induce a little anxiety and get yourself up to your peak level. But be sure that you understand yourself and your situation before you do.

Your self-confidence may vary greatly from day to day, match to match, and opponent to opponent. It is quite possible to be fully confident and relaxed against one opponent and completely lacking in confidence and uptight against a different opponent, or even the same opponent on another day. This is why, of course, you have so often been told to play your own game, not your opponent's. But the issue is far more complex—you must understand yourself and how anxiety and arousal will affect your performance before you can learn to self-regulate it to maximize your performance.

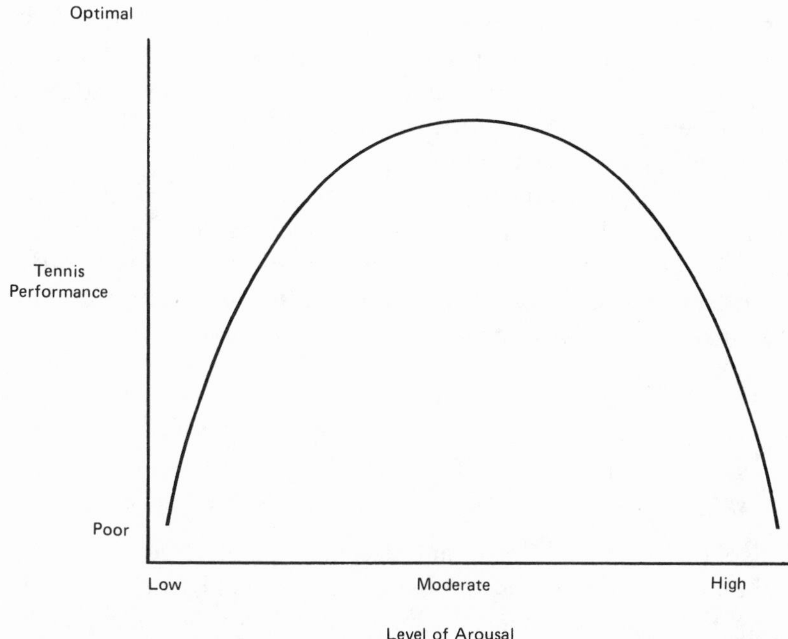

Figure 1. A moderate level of arousal will produce maximum performance. Arousal levels which are too high may produce poor performance (i.e., you clutch), while too low a level of performance produces similar negative effects (i.e., you are "not up for the match").

TENNIS ANXIETY

Understanding yourself and your emotional reactions related to tennis is an important step necessary to improving both your play and your enjoyment. If you have a tendency to worry excessively before or during a tennis game, you are no doubt playing below your potential.

Before you play a match, do you feel your heartbeat increase? Do you talk to yourself negatively and bemoan each missed shot or lost point? If you start to lose, do you grip your racket tighter and tighter? If so, you may need to learn to control your anxiety.

Psychologically, anxiety may develop when you become fearful of losing, making a mistake, or embarrassing yourself. If you can learn to control your anxiety and focus your attention purposefully, your tennis game will improve.

On page 77 is a simple self-assessment inventory for judging your anxiety level. Find a quiet place and determine if the statements reflect the way you feel.

If your score is average or above average, you will benefit from understanding your own reactions to stress and learning to control them. Carefully evaluate your own responses to the preceding questions and apply the following techniques to learning to control your anxious thoughts and improving your tennis game.

CYBERNETICS

One of the most well-documented aspects of motor performance is the understanding that the body is controlled by the mind. If you wish to master or control your tennis strokes, you must know how to tell the body to swing.

The science of cybernetics has great potential for teaching tennis players how to maximize their potential. Far too many of our current practices tend to limit our potential. Cybernetics concerns the similarities between the functioning of the human brain and nervous system and that of computers. Cybernetic study has taught us that our brains and nervous systems make up a complex, goal-striving mechanism. Depending on how we operate this automatic guidance system, it can work for us as a success mechanism or against us as a failure mechanism. If a tennis player wishes to plan for success, he should present the brain with positive or success-oriented goals. These goals of course need to be realistic, and you must be willing to practice and progress a little bit at a time. If you present the brain and nervous system with negative or failure-oriented goals, it will function as a failure mechanism.

Your automatic guidance system operates much like a computer-guided machine. Compare your forehand drive to a very sophisticated guided missile. Both have a goal, in the hitting of a target, both (if correctly programmed) have been pro-

GAT: GAUGING ANXIETY IN TENNIS

Instructions: Circle the response which most agrees with your response to the situation described next to it.

Situation	*Strongly Agree*	*Mildly Agree*	*Mildly Disagree*	*Strongly Disagree*
1. On important shots my hands are cold and I lose my feel.	4	3	2	1
2. On important serves I rush my shot even though I am not set.	4	3	2	1
3. During tournaments I try "new" shots which I have never consistently practiced.	4	3	2	1
4. When I am distracted before my serve I stop, take a deep breath, and then serve.	1	2	3	4
5. If I lose the first few games, I tend to have great difficulty throughout the match.	4	3	2	1
6. If I have to hit a backhand overhead, I cringe before I even hit it.	4	3	2	1
7. When I have an opportunity to hit an overhead to win a match I relax and can successfully hit it.	1	2	3	4
8. I am very critical of myself.	4	3	2	1
9. When the wind is blowing in my face, I grip my racket tighter than normal.	4	3	2	1
10. There are certain shots I would rather never hit.	4	3	2	1

Scoring the GAT: To determine your total score, simply add up the total of all numbers you have circled.

Maximum Score = 40 My Total Score ________

Zone	*Score*	*Tension Level*
A	40–36	Considerably Above Average in Tension
B	35–29	Above Average
C	28–21	Average
D	20–14	Below Average
E	13–10	Considerably Below Average in Tension

grammed for success, both have machinery to achieve the goal—you the tennis player, with your senses of sight, touch, and hearing, and your brain and nervous system made up of billions of nerve cells, each one with its own wiring of axons, dendrites, and synapses; the computer with its heat and pressure sensors all connected to a mass of electrical wiring. Both use feedback data carried through the system by electrical impulses, and both can use and store data in memory banks. Feedback allows the system to perform in a smooth and coordinated manner.

Every time you experience something, you either create new neural pathways or patterns in your brain or strengthen those neural pathways or patterns which already exist. These patterns are stored (like magnetic tapes in computers) and can be replayed whenever a past experience is recalled. Your job is to learn how to replay the successful experiences rather than the negative ones, therefore strengthening them to such a degree that they become automatic movements. Programming for this automatic response is what planning for success in tennis is all about.

The human brain and nervous system cannot differentiate between a real and an imagined experience. Research in sport psychology and motor learning has consistently demonstrated the superiority of combining mental practice with physical practice in both the learning and mastery of athletic skills.

The best way to successfully acquire the desired neural pathways is through the use of mental rehearsal and positive visual imagery. Mental rehearsal is typically most useful in the learning phase. These techniques can be used any time that you are learning a new shot or making a change in your strokes. When practicing mental rehearsal you should study your picture of your stroke and thoroughly analyze it part by part, over and over again. It is just as important, however, that you feel your strokes—try to cue in on the proprioceptive feedback that you get. Continually analyze and correct until you have the picture and feel that it is right.

As you learn a stroke and can consistently repeat the swing smoothly in practice, visually imagine yourself as vividly as possible stroking the ball. Be sure to imagine a wide variety of situations. Remember, at this point you are preparing yourself to be relaxed and confident in the competitive situation. The more visual practice you do and the more experience of having been there before, the more confident you will be. Visual imagery should be used on a regular basis for any shot in which you are not completely confident, e.g., hitting a high, bouncing backhand or an overhead, shagging a lob, or controlling a drop shot. If you really want to be good, be willing to spend the little time required to plan for confidence when competing in possible anxiety-producing situations.

PHYSICAL EFFECTS OF AROUSAL

The physiological effects of anxiety and the fight-or-flight response have already been described. In addition, the possible positive benefits of calling on adrenaline at just the right time have been described. For most tennis players, anxiety will be detrimental to the game.

Lack of "Feel" and Coordination

Anxiety leads to muscle tension beyond appropriate levels. Suddenly you may find that a usually smooth and coordinated stroke becomes quick and uncoordinated, or that you attempt to guide the shot. "To fear is to steer." The simultaneous contraction of agonistic muscles and relaxation of antagonistic muscles no longer automatically takes place. For example, due to the inability to relax antagonistic muscles you cannot completely extend body parts that normally extend easily when they are relaxed. Thus you lose your follow-through and relaxed finish.

Because of the decrease in blood flow to the fingers and hands when tight, the anxious tennis player loses that all-important feel that has been emphasized by so many great tennis instructors. You instead grip the racket with the classic "death grip" so hazardous to your tennis strokes. Without feel, you suddenly lose rhythm and touch on finesse shots. In other words, anxiety prevents your body from doing what it knows how to do.

Fatigue

Because your muscles tend to stay tense for prolonged periods and at inappropriate times, you will be much more susceptible to fatigue. Do you ever find that your shoulders and upper back are sore after playing? They will certainly tire easily if they never relax and recover. Combine this problem with the fight-or-flight effects on the breathing process and you quickly understand the problem and why you may also be more susceptible to injury. Suddenly it becomes clear that good tennis players know what they are doing when they take deep, slow breaths between points and prior to hitting and planning shots.

"Unlock your mind" to better tennis.

As is obvious by this point, anxiety is not good for your game. You must be aware of your anxiety-related tendencies and understand their relationship to performance. Finally, and of equal if not more importance, is the fact that anxiety is learned. Therefore, you can learn to control and eliminate it and thereby improve your tennis.

ASSESSING YOUR OWN ANXIETY TO INCREASE SELF-AWARENESS

A very simple and yet effective method of assessing anxiety in tennis is to become more aware of your own thinking style. Because anxiety is a psychological state, your thinking will tell you a great deal about whether you are anxious or self-confident. Following your next important tennis match, sit down in a quiet place and answer the following questions as honestly as possible:

1. What were your thoughts the day before the match? Did you fully expect to win or play well? Did negative thoughts often cross your mind? Were you worried about a particular stroke that has given you trouble in the past? Did you worry that the wind would be blowing and you would play poorly? Did you fear that your serve would fail you?

(Write down your thoughts as you remember them. The anxious thoughts suggest that you need to spend more time in the future on both physical and mental practice on those aspects of your game. If you lacked confidence, concentrate on your self-efficacy training.)

2. When did you feel the most anxious? Before your first serve? After hitting an overhead out of bounds? Were you positive that you could recover, or did you question your ability to do so? What did you say to yourself prior to the last three points of the breaker? Did you worry about missing? Did you wonder what your friends or partner would think if you lost? Or won!

If you can become increasingly self-aware of these specific problem areas, you will be better able to apply the mastery and coping rehearsals where they are most necessary. The previous self-assessment inventory for gauging anxiety may help you recognize potential problem areas.

If possible, it can be quite effective to videotape your play in a number of matches. Then play back the tape and, while viewing yourself, record your inner thoughts. Again, the key is to want to understand your mental deficiencies, realize that they *can* be improved, and use the described techniques to do so.

SELF-COACHING FOR YOUR MIND AND BODY

Most tennis players will have to learn how to best direct their thoughts in order to maximize their performance. Unlike other athletes, you will not have a coach taking care of your mental preparation. You will have to learn how to think for yourself.

Perhaps the most influential and useful way of controlling your mind and body is through control of self-statements. Your self-talk or the things that you say to yourself while you are competing have a significant impact upon your ability to play.

Your self-talk is particularly important in a sport like tennis. There is a great amount of time between shots for you to think (between points, sets, and matches). These thoughts appear to have a very direct impact upon how well and consistently you are able to play.

A tennis match may last from an hour to three-and-a-half hours. That is a lot of time to do a lot of thinking. If you add to it the thoughts you have prior to and following an important match, the time period is greatly extended. Clearly, the better you directly control these thoughts, the better your play will become.

You must be willing to master your self-talk. Without it your mental game will lag far behind your physical game. As a result your competitive performance will lag far behind your potential.

The first step to mastery of your self-talk involves increasing your awareness of your self-talk. Perhaps while reading this section you don't even think that you do indeed talk to yourself. The next time you play tennis pay attention to your self-talk. Listen carefully to what you say to yourself prior to, during, and following competition. After playing, carefully analyze your thoughts. Use the questions below to help you:

Prior to playing

Did you worry a lot about playing poorly?

Did you have negative thoughts?

Did you have positive thoughts?

Were your anxieties rational or irrational?

Did you just worry, or did you plan a strategy that would help you?

Were your anxieties relevant to maximal performance, or irrelevant (such as worrying about what others think, etc.)?

Did you try to make up excuses for playing poorly or avoiding competing altogether?

Were your thoughts self-encouraging or self-discouraging?

Were you looking forward to the match as an exciting challenge?

Were you depressed and fearful of how your skills would hold up under pressure?

During play

Did you think of watching the ball?

Did you dwell on winning or losing?

Did you put yourself down or build yourself up?

Did you have thoughts that were unrelated to tennis (work to do, errands to run, plans for evening, etc.)?

What were your thoughts when you were playing well?

What were your thoughts when you were missing shots or behind in the match?

When you made errors were you critical of yourself?

Did you tend to think positive or relevant thoughts when you played well and negative or irrelevant thoughts when you played poorly?

Following play

Did you put yourself down?

Did you wonder if tennis is worth the effort?

Did you consider quitting tennis?
Did you feel embarrassed about your play?
Did you stay cool and rationally analyze your strengths and weaknesses?
Did you feel depressed long after playing?
Did you feel excited over your play?
Did you take pride in how hard you tried and how much you are improving?

Once you become increasingly aware of thoughts which are inappropriate and detrimental to your concentration you must be able to change them. You will find it effective to utilize the cue word "stop" whenever you realize that your self-talk is headed in the wrong direction. Once you "stop" the negative or inappropriate thoughts, you need to repeat a simple cue word to help you relax. Cues such as "smile," "easy," or "let go" are very useful. These words are similar to the cues used in relaxation training. But it is important that you pick a cue word that will remind *you* to relax, so don't hesitate to pick your own.

Once you have stopped your thoughts and induced relaxation and quieted your mind and body, you must direct your thoughts. To do so effectively you must know what you should be thinking. This has been detailed earlier in the section on concentration. But in general you must decide upon what your strategy will be and then repeat the word "ball . . . ball . . . ball . . ." until your mind totally focuses on the ball.

The objective is to eventually concentrate and hit the ball so well that you eventually slip into the "zone" where your mind is totally absorbed in the ball. This is the state you will be searching for in tennis. When you get there you will not be forcing yourself to think "ball." You will not need to do this. You mind will just naturally attend to the ball. But when you realize that you have come out of the zone and begun struggling again, go back to your conscious mind control strategy "ball . . . ball . . . ball . . ." until you once again are totally immersed in the "zone."

Keep in mind that performance during the consciously controlled mind state is not as desirable as the ideal unconscious state. But it is far superior to the conscious negative state that occurs when your thoughts respond to negative play. In this state your self-talk becomes very distracting and self-limiting. A major goal of mind control strategies is to avoid this state of mind.

Keep in mind as we continue that many fine players have anxious or negative thoughts enter their mind. The key is to keep them from controlling and dominating your mind. When used in an appropriate manner they can be quite useful. They can be valuable cues to signal your need to cope. So when they enter your mind turn them into a source of power—a trigger for mind control. "Stop," "smile," "let go," and think "ball." When you do this, anxious thoughts will not be so scary and negative thoughts will not be self-defeating and distracting.

SELF-TALK

Your self-talk can work for or against you in a variety of ways. The better you understand the different situations where controlling your self-talk can help you, the better you will play—particularly under competitive stress.

Your *mood* is extremely important to how well you will perform. You will perform better when you are excited about playing. You will enjoy the thrill of competition and get more enjoyment out of tennis when you are elated rather than depressed. Your mood is undoubtedly influenced by the statements you make to yourself. So the next time you are preparing for a match listen carefully to thoughts which are likely to deflate your spirits; "stop" them and insert helpful self-talk such as: "I'm really looking forward to this match," "This is the best player I've ever competed against," "The match will be a great opportunity to test my skills," "I am filled with energy," "I love the feeling I get when it's time to compete."

You should also listen carefully to the way you treat yourself. If you must be critical of yourself, do so in practice, not during competition. Use your self-talk to praise and reward yourself. During competition actively seek out skills executed correctly and then praise yourself: "nice shot," "I am really playing well now," "Keep it up—I am thinking well and moving smoothly." If you are a player who tends to be overly critical of yourself, you may have to really work at this skill. It probably will not come easily to you. Learn to control your mind and become much more positive with yourself when you compete.

During the course of competition many other situations will occur which can be influenced by your self-talk. Many players get ahead in a match and tend to start thinking about getting or losing a lead. Such problems may most typically occur when you are playing someone you have never beaten before or someone you have never lost to before. Check yourself carefully. If you tend to think ahead to how great you will feel if you win or how embarrassed you will feel if you lose, prepare yourself. Get ready to recognize and stop such thoughts before they distract you, and focus your mind in the present and play one point at a time. Remember, it is OK to think in the future or past between points, games, or sets for a moment, but when it's time to play your mind must *focus in the present and on the ball.*

Another key time to check self-critical self-talk is after an error. Pros make the same errors every day and remain calm. They do so to help them concentrate on how they will hit the shot correctly the next time they need to hit it. It makes no sense for you to be self-critical if a pro who spends hours every day practicing makes the same error.

It does make sense on occasion to be critical. Sometimes it may even help your concentration. When you are underaroused, bored, or asleep on a shot, then it may be useful to criticize yourself and remind yourself to concentrate. But this case is indeed an exception rather than a rule.

Some players have just the opposite problem of overly critical players. They play well and suddenly their attention drifts to thinking about how well they are playing. Although this problem may not be as self-defeating as critical thinking, it is distracting and hinders performance. Most players will experience this problem occasionally and must make certain that it does not detract from performance.

Any situation which is likely to have an *emotional* impact can lead to negative self-talk. You must be certain to control your mind in these situations. It really doesn't matter if it is a bad line call, missing an extremely easy shot that embarrasses you, double-faulting, or feeling sorry for yourself when things are going against you. The key is recognizing that the emotion will induce self-defeating self-talk and therefore limit your performance.

A WORD OF CAUTION

Mind control through control of your self-talk will not occur overnight. It will take time and patience to truly understand your mind. At first becoming aware of your thoughts may even be distracting. So practice in your fun matches where there is little pressure. As you become more skilled at controlling your self-talk your confidence will improve as you are better able to control your mind and your body.

Many tennis players experience specific anxieties which will work against their performance. Specific anxieties must be faced and overcome. To do otherwise would be hazardous to your game.

You should not feel inferior because you have these anxieties. Almost everyone has them. Even a player such as Chris Evert Lloyd has had to learn to conquer her fear of the net. It should be obvious that if the best players in the world admit having problems and work to overcome them, then it should be all right for you.

ASSESSMENT OF YOUR SELF-TALK

Do your thoughts work for you, or against you? Learn to turn your self-defeating thoughts into self-enhancing ones.

Self-Defeating	*Self-Enhancing*
1. There is no sense in practicing and trying to improve. I have no talent and could never be any good anyway.	1. I have seen many effective tennis players who seem to have very average physical abilities. With my attitude and desire I can get better if I practice correctly.

Self-Defeating	*Self-Enhancing*
2. I'd like to improve my tennis but I don't have time. My work and family require too much of my time.	2. I'd like to improve my tennis game. I need to schedule my time more effectively. Maybe I can go into work an hour earlier or occasionally take my spouse or children with me to play tennis.
3. I'm too old to start trying to improve my tennis. People will laugh and think I am foolish to put so much time and effort into a game.	3. Tennis should be a great game for someone my age. People will really admire me if I get better and improve my game. I will get a chance to interact with people of all ages and make new friends. It will help keep me feeling young.
4. The only way to get good at tennis is to have a lot of money so you can have great lessons. This has been true for anyone who is good. I wish I were born rich and lucky.	4. To get good at tennis I will need quality lessons. On my budget I will have to set aside some money each week or give up something I don't really need so that I can get them. I must find a solution.
5. I don't think that I will try hard to improve my tennis. If I try and fail to get better, I will look bad and people will think that I must really be lacking in talent.	5. I will try hard to improve my tennis. I'm sure I can get better. But no matter what happens I will find out what my potential is. I will know that I gave it my best shot. I will never have to regret that I didn't at least try.

If you really wish to change your self-talk and learn to control your anxieties, you must be willing to work at it. You cannot always change your environment, but you can always change your reaction to it, by practicing the three basic steps in the change process.

THREE BASIC STEPS IN THE CHANGE PROCESS FOR ANXIETY SELF-CONTROL

STEP 1: *Self-Observation or Guided Interview*

Increased sensitivity—heightened awareness
Deliberate attention
Self-monitoring

Thoughts—images—self-talk
Physiological reactions
Interpersonal behaviors
Athlete reconceptualizes problem

STEP 2: *Eliminating Incompatible Thoughts and Behaviors*

Produce adaptive thoughts (images and self-statements)
Produce adaptive behaviors
Interfere with maladaptive thoughts
Identify and practice appropriate self-statements and thoughts
Prior to performance
During performance
Following performance

STEP 3: *Changing Beliefs about New Behaviors*

Alter cognitive structures
Change self-perception of reaction-nonreaction of significant others
Modify cognitions and behaviors in everyday situations and future sport situations
Modify self-assessment of the new behavioral outcomes
Assure maintenance and generalization of new thoughts and behaviors

---

CONQUERING NET ANXIETY

Consider, for example, the fear and anxiety that many people have relative to playing at the net. Do you find yourself making up reasons not to develop a net game? Do you come in to hit short balls and then turn and sprint to the baseline? If your answer is yes, you have probably built up an anxiety about coming to the net. It is time to do something about it. Start thinking of as many reasons as you can for learning to play the net. Next you must go to work on your confidence. As Chris Evert Lloyd stated after overcoming her own fear at the net: "Conquering fear of the net is all a matter of confidence, really. I found that once I broke through the confidence barrier, I was fine!"

Conquering fear and developing self-confidence can be learned.

The approach outlined is very similar to the one utilized by Lloyd. It is based on sound psychological strategies. It will require you to be motivated and patient.

You have probably built up a wide variety of negative self-statements anytime you even think about going to net. You will need to stop these thoughts whenever they occur. From now on anytime that you go to net repeat one of the following self-statements to yourself: "step to ball" or "move foward." These are appropriate thoughts that will direct your attention.

Next, you must break down the skill into its parts. Begin by standing a few feet from the net without your racket. Ask a friend to *throw* (not hit) a number of balls to you. Have some balls thrown to your right and some to your left. Catch them. When you are comfortable and realize that you can catch the ball at the net you will be ready to have your partner throw balls straight at your body. Tell your friend to throw the balls as slowly as you desire. Gradually have your friend throw the balls a little bit faster. Now step to the ball and move more to the sides.

Now, at your own pace, have the balls thrown farther away from your body, so that you must take one, two, and then three steps to catch the ball. Once again, start out slowly and gradually increase the speed of the ball and repeat to yourself, "step to ball," to prevent anxious thoughts from entering your mind. Do the above drills until you are completely relaxed and comfortable while doing them. It is perfectly acceptable to use a Nerf Ball if you find that you are initially afraid of the tennis ball.

Now, you are ready to repeat the same drills with your tennis racket. Your partner still throws the ball where you want it, at the speed that you desire. You decide when to ask your partner to increase the distance or speed of the ball toss, or you tell your partner when to advance to throwing the balls to you overhand and faster. You tell your partner when to advance to throwing balls to you at random. You tell your friend when you are ready to have the balls *hit* to you rather than thrown to you. Remember to repeat, "step to ball," and make sure that you are comfortable before you advance to the next step. It does not matter how rapidly you progress. The key is to build a number of successes that will help you develop confidence each step of the way. As you gain in confidence, stand near the net and try to volley right back to your partner so that you can begin to develop control. This will further add to your confidence.

Gradually move farther away from the net until you can comfortably hit volleys from behind the service line. When you can do so without anxiety for several sessions it is time for you to prepare to hit an approach shot and volley combination. Begin by standing about three feet behind the service line with a ball in your hand. Place your partner in the same position at the opposite end of the court with a ball in hand. You hit a ball over the net and down the line and *walk* toward the net. As your ball lands have your partner throw a ball to a predetermined side of your body. You "step to ball" and volley the shot. Repeat this many times until you feel comfortable.

From here you must simply advance to the point where your partner hits a short groundstroke, you run to the ball and hit an approach shot, follow it to net, anticipate the return, and then "step to ball."

SERVE AND VOLLEY

A very similar process is useful for learning to serve and volley. Begin by serving and walking to the service line behind your serve until you are comfortable moving foward after your serve. When you're ready, have your friend throw a ball to your side as you near the service line. You must continue "step to ball" and hitting the volley. Gradually pick up your pace and the pace at which the return of serve is thrown or hit to you. Eventually serve and volley full speed with returns hit at random. When you have accomplished this, it is time to try your skill in a modified game. You and your partner plan a set in which you both *must always* serve and volley. The person returning serve cannot lob but must try, at least initially, to hit returns right to the server in the middle of the court. You can modify the rules however you wish, but remember the objective—you are working to learn how to volley. Winning is not important now.

You should now be ready to try your new skills in a real game. Find an opponent that you can usually beat. Do not tell him that you are working on your volley. Commit yourself ahead of time to play *at least the first set* using a serve-and-volley game and following all short balls to net. Decide that no matter what the score is you will stick with your plan. Nothing will change your mind—even a suddenly cocky opponent. Just keep reminding yourself that this strategy will pay off in the future. But be patient—it will take time.

When you are truly comfortable at net, try to line up an opponent who hits the ball hard but with control. Ask him to hit balls at you while you are at the net. Do this as much as you can until you start loving to play the net. You'll know that you are there when you start wanting to master the approach shot and develop your overhead.

The program just outlined is designed to insure that you will develop a volley. It will be helpful to visualize each exercise in your head several times before you try them. This program will work if you follow it, take your time, remain persistent, and repeat "step to ball" or "move forward." The approach is based on a sound psychological principle known as systematic desensitization which has been utilized for years for managing phobias such as snake phobia or fear of heights.

6
Eliminating Inappropriate Muscle Tension

Many tennis players fail to understand the detrimental effects of inappropriate muscle tension or lack knowledge concerning what to do about it. Much too often, its effects are not even considered.

When tension and anxiety cause you problems, or when frequently missed shots cause you anxiety problems, relax and focus on the total pattern of the stroke, not the specifics. One of the first symptoms of increased anxiety may be the *iron grip.* Many people start gripping their rackets tighter and tighter. To alleviate this it might be helpful to roll your fingers, spin your racket in your hand, or switch it to the other hand while changing courts.

Worry and anxiety may also affect your strokes. Unfortunately, at this level, it may be harmful to focus on these strokes. Instead, attention should be directed to the total feel of the stroke in order to make it possible for the strokes to be "run off" automatically. For example, it may be helpful to think about keeping your feet moving, because if they are in position, the opportunity to stroke the ball well will be enhanced. Another strategy includes focusing on the perception of the ball by saying such things as "bounce stroke" or "think ball."

Many tennis instructors will emphasize the importance of the contraction of certain muscle groups which are required to execute a particular shot. However, far too many players are hurt by contracting these muscles too tightly, the result being ineffective and inconsistent performance. Unfortunately, most tennis players are at a loss when it comes to eliminating excess tension. Frequently our only response is to yell at ourselves, "RELAX!" Naturally because we have not practiced how to do so, and are well aware that we cannot yet control tension, our brains send messages to the body indicating anxiety over the excess tension, which only increases muscle tension.

Any time a tennis stroke is executed, there are two muscle groups which must be controlled for a smooth, coordinated movement. Too frequently we concern ourselves with the main movers, known as the agonistic muscles. But in order to have a coordinated and efficient stroke, the opposite muscle group (the antagonistic muscles) must simultaneously relax. Unfortunately, when we "choke" in tennis, it is usually the result of our inability to identify and control inappropriate muscle tension.

BREATH CONTROL

The fact that the whole concept of tightness during performance can be identified by the term "choke" (which relates to breathing) tells you something about its importance. Masters of the martial arts have long understood the relevance of breath control to tension management. Certainly in recent years anyone familiar with the Lamaze natural childbirth techniques realizes the value of breath control to muscle relaxation. This technique can facilitate relaxation and exercise control over the fight-or-flight syndrome.

A deep, slow breath in a stressful situation tells the brain that the body is back in control. The result is cessation of the fight-or-flight response, which naturally leads to muscular relaxation.

Many successful tennis players have learned to prevent excess pressure or tension by simply taking a couple of deep, slow breaths any time that they anticipate a stressful situation. Take a deep breath yourself and feel the relaxed feeling that comes over

Release the pressures of tennis. Learn to control your mind and body.

your body during and following exhalation. This is the reason why the relaxed player should continue to breathe during stroke execution.

It is well recognized that because of the increased relaxed state resulting from a forced exhalation, the power of your serve can be increased. This certainly explains the grunts of the big servers such as McEnroe, Tanner, and Navratilova.

A final point should be emphasized. The benefit of rhythmic breathing will not be realized while you are *thinking* about breathing. It must become a relaxed and automatic behavior.

COMPLETE AND DIFFERENTIAL RELAXATION

Mastering the sport of tennis requires not only mastery of muscle contraction but also mastery of muscle relaxation. Indeed, it is the correct relaxation that distinguishes the skillful player from the uncoordinated one. As a matter of fact, coordination is correct differential relaxation. The ineffective stroke of the poor tennis player is caused by either (1) contracting too forcefully muscles requiring slight degrees of contraction or (2) contracting muscles which should be relaxed to produce a smooth stroke.

It is helpful to understand the difference between complete and differential relaxation. Complete relaxation means zero activity of the voluntary muscles of the body. The normal tone of the muscles will not be visible. Complete muscle relaxation is extremely useful for inducing sleep and for gaining greater self-awareness of muscle relaxation. Differential relaxation means differentiating between muscles that are necessary for an activity and those that are not. Relaxing muscles that are not needed in the performance of a shot is essential for differential relaxation. Differential relaxation also means differentiating between strong and weak contractions of the required muscles and relaxing them as much as is consistent with doing the job at hand effectively. Thus for mastery of tennis, differential relaxation should be practiced continually in connection with a wide variety of daily activities in addition to movements demanded in tennis.

COMPLETE BODY RELAXATION

The first phase of learning to relax while playing tennis is to increase your self-awareness of the difference between various degrees of muscle relaxation and tension. Clearly, in order to eliminate tension you must increase your sensitivity to its presence so that you will recognize it and then control it. The following exercises have been developed to help in this process. As you practice them, feel for areas of your body where you have the most difficulty eliminating tension. These areas may require special practice because it is most likely that they will cause you problems in your tennis stroke.

Body Relaxation Exercises

While practicing the following exercises, focus your attention on the way your body feels. If your mind wanders onto other thoughts, calmly tell yourself "stop," push those thoughts away, and concentrate on your bodily feelings.

These exercises have two major functions: (1) to teach you to recognize muscle tension and muscle relaxation so that you will become more aware of them and (2) to teach you to eliminate muscle tension once you recognize it and to be able to induce relaxation.

Find a quiet place where you can lie down for about fifteen to twenty minutes each day for the next two weeks. Lie down on your back and make yourself comfortable. (You may wish to place a pillow under your neck and/or knees.) Place your arms at your side, with your fingers open. Close your eyes. Do not force them shut. Hold them comfortably closed. Tense all of the muscles in the lower part of your body from your hips to the tip of your toes. Point your toes away from your body with your heels about four to six inches apart. Tighten the muscles in your calves, thighs, and buttocks. Feel the tension as you hold it. Remember this feeling. Slowly count: "1 . . . 2 . . . 3 . . . 4 . . . ," then say the words "let go" to yourself and slowly let the tension flow out of your body. Again concentrate on calves, thighs, and buttocks. Let your toes point upward and flop to the outside. Feel the relaxation. Remember how good it feels. Feel the heaviness and the warmth flowing through the lower body. Let it feel good. If you have any tension anywhere in your lower body, "let go."

Now concentrate on your stomach. Tighten it as much as you can. Feel the tension as you hold it. Remember the feeling. Count "1 . . . 2 . . . 3 . . . 4 . . . ," repeat the words "let go" to yourself, and slowly let the tension flow out of your body. Again, concentrate on your stomach muscles. Feel the relaxation. Remember how good it feels. Let it feel good for a moment. If there is any tension anywhere in your body, let it go.

Concentrate on your chest muscles. Tighten your chest

muscles as tightly as you can. Take a deep breath through your mouth and then hold it. As you hold it you may feel tension spots in your chest. Remember where they are—they may surface on the tennis court. Now slowly "let go"—very slowly. Breathe normally and comfortably as if you were sleeping or resting. Make sure you have eliminated the tension spots. Relax your whole body completely.

Tighten all the muscles from the tips of your fingers to your shoulders in both arms as tightly as you can. Raise your arms about a foot off the floor. Clench your fists. Feel the tension throughout your fingers, hands, arms, and shoulders. Hold it. Count "1 . . . 2 . . . 3 . . . 4 . . ." and feel the tension. Slowly "let go." Let your arms drop and your fingers spread, and completely relax. Feel your hands and arms. If there is any remaining tension, remember where it is. You are likely to get tension there while playing tennis in a stressful situation. Now, "let go" and completely relax.

Once again, concentrate on just your fingers. Relax them completely. Feel how warm and heavy they are. Relax your upper arms completely. Eliminate any excess tension.

Now concentrate on the muscles of your upper back—the muscles between the shoulder blades and the neck. These muscles are very sensitive to tension. You may have experienced soreness here after a tournament. Tighten these muscles as much as possible. Feel the tension and hold it. Count "1 . . . 2 . . . 3 . . . 4 . . . ," then slowly "let go." Dwell on the feelings of relaxation as you do so. Concentrate on these relaxed feelings and remember them.

Now tighten your entire body as tightly as you can from the tips of your fingers to the top of your toes. Hold it: "1 . . . 2 . . . 3 . . . 4 . . . ," slowly "let go," and completely relax your entire body. If you have any residual tension remaining anywhere in your body, let it go.

Imagine a pleasant scene, like walking on a beach or lying in a rowboat on a calm pond—any place where you feel completely relaxed. Let your whole body feel calm and relaxed. Enjoy the feelings. Take a couple of very deep, slow breaths. Inhale deeply into your stomach: "1 . . . 2 . . . 3 . . . 4 . . . ," and then exhale slowly, "1 . . . 2 . . . 3 . . . 4 . . . ." Feel your body get more and more relaxed. Breathe normally, smoothly, and calmly. Continue to feel your body and let go of any remaining tension.

Differential Relaxation Techniques

Focus your attention on your right arm (or left, if you hold the racket in the left hand). Contract the muscles of your right arm and wrist. Make a fist. Feel the tightness from your shoulder to the tips of your fingers. Keep all the other muscles of your body relaxed and breathe normally.

As you tense the right side feel the difference between your right and left side of your body. Feel your legs. Do you have any tension remaining in your legs? If you do, let it go. Keep the whole body relaxed while maintaining a tense right arm. Count "1 . . . 2 . . . 3 . . . 4 . . . ." Now relax your right arm also. That's it—let the whole body feel relaxed and calm. Keep breathing.

Repeat the process with the muscles of your left arm and hand; totally relax the rest of your body.

Focus your attention on your left arm and your right leg. Tighten them as much as you can while keeping all the other muscles of your body completely relaxed. Feel your body. Is there tension in your right arm? Let it go completely. Is there any tension in your left leg? Let it go completely.

Gradually let the tension go in your left arm and right leg. Stop at different degrees of tension along the way. Keep the left arm and right leg one-half tense while relaxing all other muscles totally. Relax to one-third tense. Keep breathing smoothly and rhythmically. Now relax your whole body.

Focus your attention on your dominant hand. Squeeze these fingers into the palms of your hands. Feel your hand. If there is still tension, let it go. Feel your lower and upper arm. Feel your bicep and tricep. Are they relaxed or is there tension? Let some of the tension go in your little fingers. Relax a little more. Imagine you are holding a baby bird or an egg with your little fingers. Keep the rest of your body relaxed.

Now totally relax your whole body.

Focus your attention on your shoulders. Shrug both shoulders up toward your ears, and hold them there. Feel the tension in the back of your shoulders. Totally relax the rest of your body. Continue to breathe smoothly and regularly. Slowly release the tension in your shoulders and relax your whole body.

Now shrug your shoulders up to your ears again, while keeping the rest of your body relaxed. Relax and lower your right shoulder only. Completely relax the right shoulder while maintaining tension in the left. Focus on the relaxed feelings in the left shoulder and the tension in the right.

Focus your attention on your left shoulder. Raise it slightly and feel the tension in the back of your left shoulder. Completely relax your right shoulder and the rest of your body. Breathe smoothly and regularly. Count "1 . . . 2 . . . 3 . . . 4 . . ." Slowly let go and relax your whole body.

Stretch your whole body slowly. Open your eyes and stand up. Assume your ready position. Place your racket in your hands and grip it. Grip the racket lightly with slight pressure in the fingers of your dominant hand.

OVERCOMING PROBLEMS IN RELAXATION TRAINING

Sometimes tennis players will experience problems in learning and practicing progressive relaxation. Most of the problems are quite common and have simple solutions.

The most typical problems (and solutions) are as follows:

1. *Noise.* Initially a quiet, darkened room is best. Later, it is a good idea to practice in an environment with light, noise, or other distractions that will be present when you are competing.

2. *Muscle cramps.* Occasionally cramps may occur in the calves, feet, neck, or lower back. Cramps may be eliminated in muscle groups that give you particular tension problems by simply generating less tension in these areas for shorter time periods.

Slowing down may also help. When cramps do occur, feel free to manipulate the cramped area before continuing.

3. *Sleep.* Unless you are specifically using relaxation training to induce sleep, sleep is not desired. Ideally you should remain awake while relaxing so that you can move from relaxation to visual imagery of your tennis performance. It can be useful to set an alarm clock for perhaps a half-hour time period. This will wake you up if you do go to sleep and keep you from worrying about going to sleep (which will distract you from the exercises). If you do the exercises late in the evening, it is easy to go to sleep afterward.

4. *Inability to relax certain muscle groups.* It is possible and normal to have certain muscle groups that will not relax very easily. These are often the same muscles that athletes have trouble relaxing during competition. You will find that if you will patiently work on slowing down or exercising troublesome muscle groups, you can usually learn to relax them.

Remember that relaxation training can teach you a great deal about yourself and your muscle tension. You may find that when you have had a stressful day you will not be able to relax as readily as usual. Realize that you do have these day-to-day fluctuations in tension levels and they can affect your performance. The self-awareness you gain can only help you on and off the court.

7
Getting the Most Out of Your Tennis Lessons

Many tennis players spend vast amounts of money on tennis instruction, but because of various psychological barriers many never get their money's worth. Often the problems are caused by personality or communication deficiencies of the instructor. If you hear from others that certain pros have such problems, then don't waste your time and money on them.

But what about the common situation where the psychological or communication barriers are the student's, that is, yours? Perhaps you go to your first lesson feeling that you are a lousy tennis player. You are quite shy and self-conscious as you approach the practice court. You start to hit a few shots to show the pro that you really are a good player. But you are trying too hard and start spraying your shots all over the place. Pretty soon you are embarrassed. You begin to imagine that the pro hates teaching such an incompetent student. Despite your teacher's good intentions to show you your problems and correct them, you are not really listening. You are more intent on showing the instructor that you really aren't such a bad player. Your lesson ends; you pay the pro and go home. The next morning you play a practice match with a friend. You discover that you learned nothing at your lesson. That does it; lessons are useless; you decide never to take another.

If this reminds you of someone you know rather well, it's time for a change. Most tennis players have the physical ability required but are not good enough students to become top-notch players. It would be very difficult to identify many players on the pro tour who have not had lessons and/or do not still receive lessons on occasion. When a pro takes a lesson, the anxieties experienced by the average or weekend player are usually absent or greatly reduced. But even at that level there are pros who are not playing up to their potential because they either don't hear or don't wish to hear the instructions from their teachers.

PICKING AN EFFECTIVE TEACHER

Try never to take a tennis lesson without finding out as much as possible about every available teacher. Talk to others who have taken lessons from them. Whenever possible, get permission to observe the prospective teacher in action. A good teacher will not be reluctant to allow you to watch. But do make sure that you are considerate of other students taking lessons. Do not distract the attention of either the teacher or the student. Stand back, out of the way, and simply observe and think. Would you enjoy taking a lesson from this teacher? Does the teacher appear to have a thorough understanding of the skills of tennis? Is the teacher organized and prepared? Does the teacher effectively communicate knowledge to the student? Is the atmosphere relaxed and conducive to learning? Or does the teacher like to destroy confidence and show off? When the teacher demonstrates correct execution of shots, is attention placed on the pertinent body parts of the instructor or on the racket? Is the teacher's main instructional comment, "Watch the ball," or does the teacher really teach?

Possibly the single most important ingredient to look for in a tennis teacher is whether the teacher builds confidence in the student's ability. Students become what their teacher expects them to become. Teachers who encourage you by emphasizing that you have ability will motivate you to practice. Obviously, if you have the ability, all you need to do is practice effectively. However, teachers who tell their students that they are lacking in coordination or strength usually suggest to their students that they should stop practicing. Let's face it, if you have no ability, what good will practice do? Research studies show that the perception communicated by the teacher to the student is more important to achievement than whether or not the student is actually talented.

Research has also made it very clear that teacher expectations have a very significant impact on the future learning and performance of each student. Teachers treat their students very differently based upon their performance expectancies. If a teacher feels that you have great potential in tennis, you may be given attention and interest. The quality of the attention also tends to be much greater.

It is quite clear that teachers make value judgments about their students. Their teaching styles often vary greatly based upon how they view each student's abilities and interests. Students evaluated favorably receive more positive feedback and are often encouraged to practice diligently.

What should be obvious by now is that students frequently become what their teachers expect them to become. Every tennis player should be aware of this inclination. Take responsibility for your own future outcome. If you have a teacher who does not get excited about teaching you and does not see you as having potential, find a new instructor. It is highly likely that your present teacher will not be the best for the future development of your game.

What happens at the end of the lesson? Does the teacher leave you feeling good about the lesson? Does the teacher identify a few key points for the student to practice? Is the student told fairly precisely how to practice? Are drills described? Is the student asked to attain a certain level of proficiency by the next lesson? Does the teacher give the student a form in writing summarizing the major points of the lesson? Such techniques will prevent the student from hearing only half the lesson due to fear of forgetting the last point the teacher made. It will also insure that the key points are not forgotten in the near future. Finally, if the teacher is the club pro, is real concern shown to students when met outside of the lesson time?

DON'T PUT UNNECESSARY PRESSURE ON YOURSELF

Far too many individuals play tennis only once or twice a week and imagine that they should be as good as the pros they see on TV. Many of these players take a few lessons from the pro and expect a miracle. This attitude will only tend to make you and your instructor frustrated. The result will be a less-than-effective lesson.

If you find that during the course of your lesson you are not fully comprehending what the teacher is telling you, do not allow yourself to be timid and worried. Speak up. Stop the instructor. Another approach may get the point across. Do not let yourself feel that you are inadequate because you did not understand the teacher. A good teacher will find a way to get the message across to you.

USING YOUR TENNIS MATCH TO DIRECT YOUR PRACTICES

Each time you play a tennis match, you should use it to indicate the relative strengths and weaknesses of your game. It is important that you have an outward focus during the match, but after each experience you should analyze your performance and plan the subsequent practices in relation to your strengths and weaknesses.

One useful technique is to carefully evaluate each match, and each game for that matter, in relation to your individual strengths and weaknesses. Analyze each stroke utilized in terms of the appropriate shot selection as well as the actual execution. For example, the following evaluation tool may be helpful in analyzing your skills.

Performing and Learning Analysis (PLAN)

The PLAN scoresheet is designed to assist you in evaluating your tennis play under game conditions. To utilize PLAN, first record the players' names in relation to the service order as soon as it has been determined. In the example provided, Sue won the spin and elected to serve first, so her name was recorded as first server.

Note that each point won is marked with an X. In Sue's case, if her first serve was good, a [1] was placed in the box. If she served a second serve and it was good, a [2] was marked. If she double-faulted, a triangle was placed in the box ◪. An ace was recorded as an [X].

Game 1 illustrates this simple system. Sue got her first or second serve in for each of the first three points and won each of those points (score = 40–love). Unfortunately, she double-faulted (◪) the next point, and lost the following rally (score = 40–30). Her next serve was good and she won that rally and the point for game 1 [X].

The games won by the player being evaluated are recorded by placing an X in the circle adjacent to the game number Ⓧ. It can be quickly observed that Sue won game 1.

In game 2, Ken served and lost the first two points. He then served an ace, followed by a double-fault (score = 15–40). Ken came back to win the next two points to the score at deuce, but double-faulted the last two points for the game.

PLAN should be used throughout at least one set in order to plot the strengths and weaknesses of a player's game. Note that in game 1 Sue did reasonably well, though when she got ahead, 40–love, she lost the next two points. If this pattern recurs, it might suggest that her attention wanders as she gains confidence. Ken, on the other hand, seems to have a problem with his serve. In game 2, he never got his first serve in, and he double-faulted three times—a sure sign of a skill which needs patient practice.

If Sue's match is followed through the first set, we can plot the game scores, and also a specific "Stroke Assessment." The next PLAN shows the entire first set for Sue and Ken's match, plus an analysis of Sue's strokes (right-side box score).

Sue's evaluator marked her PLAN each time Sue committed

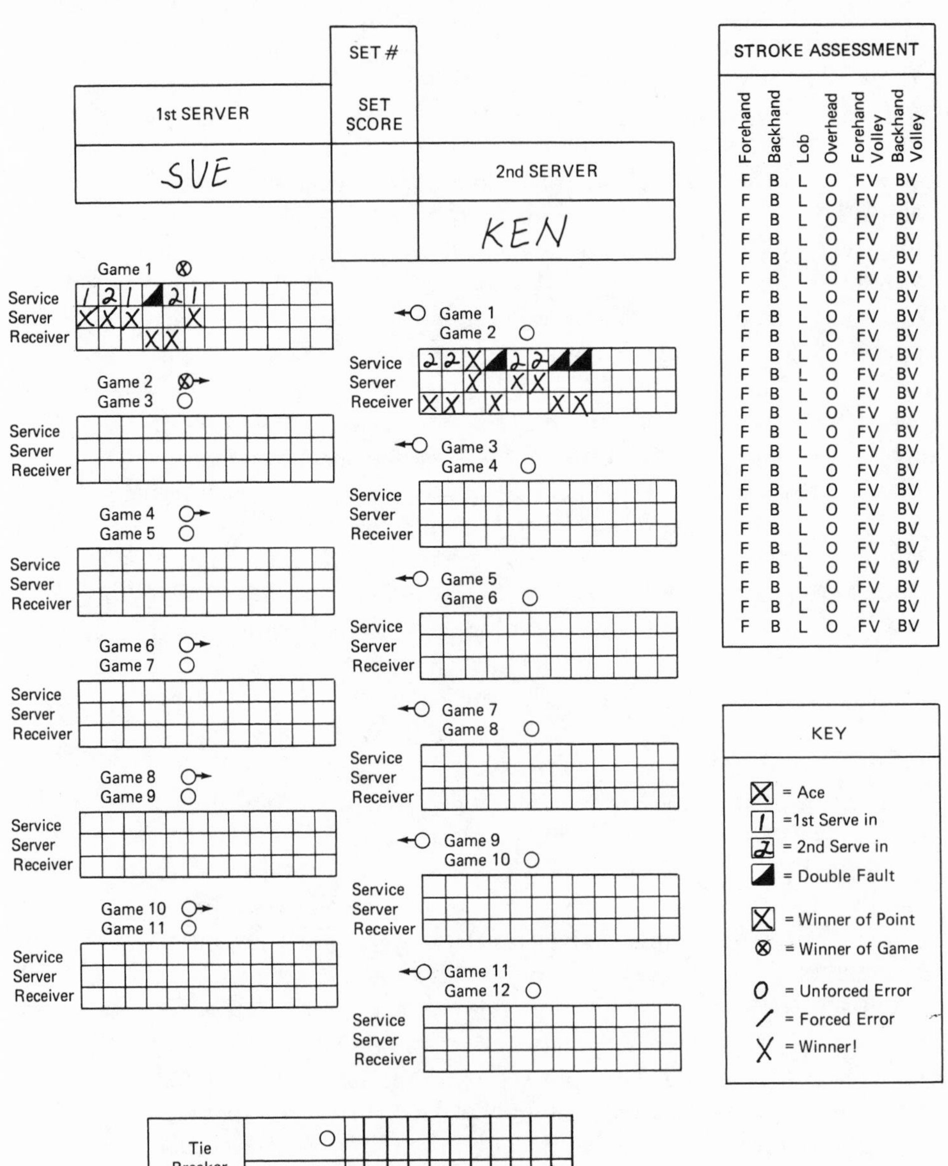
SET #
1st SERVER
SET SCORE
SUE
2nd SERVER
KEN
STROKE ASSESSMENT
Forehand
Backhand
Lob
Overhead
Forehand Volley
Backhand Volley
Game 1
Service
Server
Receiver
Game 2
Game 3
Game 4
Game 5
Game 6
Game 7
Game 8
Game 9
Game 10
Game 11
Game 12
KEY
= Ace
=1st Serve in
= 2nd Serve in
= Double Fault
= Winner of Point
= Winner of Game
= Unforced Error
= Forced Error
= Winner!
Tie Breaker

an error or won a point because of her superb shots. The Stroke Assessment portion of PLAN was marked with an X over the stroke if Sue hit a winner off a forehand, backhand, etc. A slash was placed over the appropriate letter if an error was forced because of an opponent's good play, or a circle if an unforced error occurred.

The performance recorded during set I shows that Sue has a significant problem with her backhand. She committed nine unforced errors and four forced errors from her backhand. Coupled with backhand volley errors (six), Sue has an obvious direction for her future practice sessions—backhand drills. Sue's PLAN also points out several strengths in her game, especially her overhead and forehand volley.

This PLAN can be used by Sue to identify her strengths and weaknesses and establish systematic goals for her future practices. Sue will now evaluate her serves. Does she get the first one in often enough? She will practice her backhand drive and volley, and continue to reinforce her forehand and overhead.

PLAN can and should also be used to monitor Sue's progress. Like Sue, you should have a friend or pro plot your present skills, and then use that PLAN to organize your practices. There are blank PLAN scoresheets at the end of this book for your use.

PRACTICING AFTER YOUR LESSON

Following your lesson it is an excellent idea to take your lesson review notes home and review them often. Put them in your tennis racket cover and take them with you to practice.

New tennis skills will not be mastered overnight. Patience and practice are the only answers. Do not allow yourself to play in a competitive situation until you are sure you have perfected the new techniques. Premature competition will most likely encourage you to slip back into your old strokes and bad habits because they may still feel more comfortable.

A better idea would be to practice until you feel comfortable and relaxed with your new swing. Then try to induce pressure

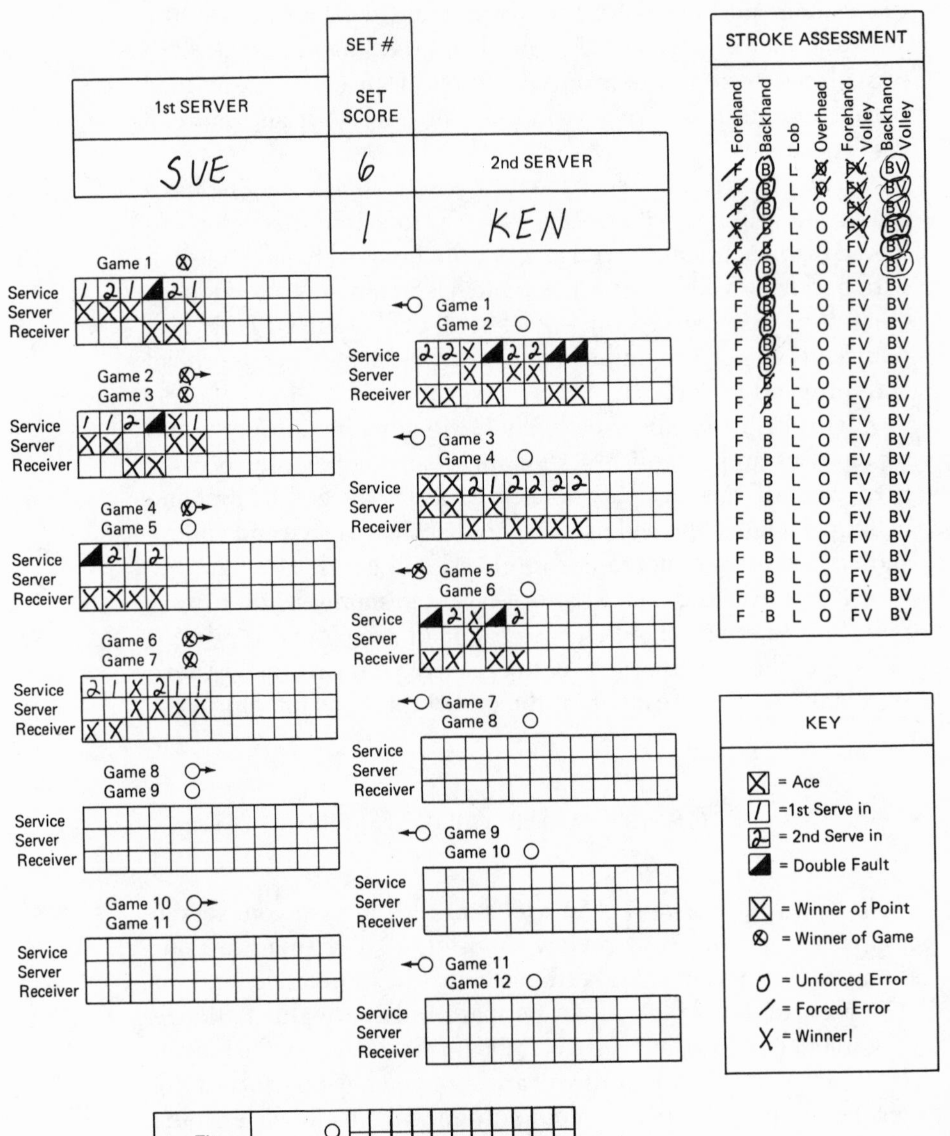
SET #
1st SERVER
SET SCORE
2nd SERVER
SUE
6
1
KEN
STROKE ASSESSMENT
Forehand
Backhand
Lob
Overhead
Forehand Volley
Backhand Volley
Game 1
Game 2
Game 3
Game 4
Game 5
Game 6
Game 7
Game 8
Game 9
Game 10
Game 11
Game 12
Service
Server
Receiver
Tie Breaker
KEY
= Ace
=1st Serve in
= 2nd Serve in
= Double Fault
= Winner of Point
= Winner of Game
= Unforced Error
= Forced Error
= Winner!

into your practice session by using competitive drills, such as counting consecutive strokes or aiming at targets. Next, play a match with someone who will help you work on your new skills. Finally, you should be ready. If you find out that you're not, don't be discouraged. Go back to practice and practice some more.

THERE IS NO SUBSTITUTE FOR HITTING TENNIS BALLS

There is absolutely no substitute for repeatedly stroking a tennis ball. You must have the proper stroke, and that must be a reproducible stroke. This consistent skill must be practiced, but the old adage "Practice makes perfect" should be carefully employed. It is actually *perfect* practice that makes perfect.

Hopefully, the ideas presented here will help you get more out of those expensive lessons. But let us remind you of one point: you will never perfect the game of tennis, so don't expect to. Even the best pros identify skills which need additional practice.

8

Getting the Most Out of Your Practice

OK, you have decided to become a maximizer in tennis! You have decided you will work to improve your weaknesses and perfect your strengths in order to become a high achiever. You are willing to become increasingly aware of the mental side of your game. You have selected the best teacher available. You have had a lesson or many lessons. How do you now combine physical and mental practice in a way that is most efficient for attaining success? Remember, if you are going to practice, your practice must be designed to maximize your payoff—improvement and success in tennis.

Right from the very start, plan your practice in a manner conducive to the formation of good habits. Habits do not change easily, so good habits will stay with you, even in pressure situations. Of course, if you form bad habits, this point still holds true: they will be difficult to change. If you establish no set practice pattern, you will not establish consistent strokes at all, and will be likely to have problems in stressful situations.

DEVELOPING GOOD, FORCEFUL STROKES

The development of confident, forceful strokes is linked directly to the amount and nature of the practice of those strokes. Individuals who have practiced consistently will be confident that their strokes will hold up in a variety of situations.

Practice the Stroke, Not Accuracy

One of the most common errors in the early stages of learning tennis is to concentrate too much on where the ball is going. Unfortunately, if you focus on accuracy, your strokes may never really develop, since accuracy is often accomplished by shortening the stroke and altering the stroke pattern. For example, you can easily remember feeling the pressure of a double-fault, followed by a desire to merely "patty-cake" the ball into the service court.

Many top teaching pros emphasize the idea that when introducing the serve, practice should not be in relation to accuracy. Instead, begin by turning your body away from the net and hitting the ball into the backstop. Do this until a smooth pattern emerges. This pattern should provide the basis for almost any serve, since the ball toss and sequential timing of the arm are the most difficult aspects of the serve.

Once the basic service motion has been acquired, focus can be shifted to the specific requirement of hitting the ball into the service box. It is critical at this time that tennis players continue to focus on good pattern development, and not just "getting it in." If you are having trouble with your serve, take time out from game play to practice it. Or alter the rules of the game so that you and your friends agree to play the first one in each time, or give three or four tries per point. After all, the rules of the game are arbitrary, and should be modified to meet *your* needs. But keep in mind that once your stroke is developed correctly and is grooved, it is time to prepare for competition. You can no longer focus attention on how to hit the ball.

MODIFY GAMES TO FACILITATE PATTERN DEVELOPMENT

The best way to acquire good tennis strokes is to practice those strokes. If you wish to focus on good, deep shots, devise a game to encourage that. For example, why not make up a game in which the object is to keep the ball deep in the opponent's court, between the service and baseline. Points would be lost for short balls, or ones which pass over the net at a height of greater than eight feet. Targets placed at the corners of the court could be used as "extra credit" or "buy a beer" goals. This "B and B" (baseline to baseline) game provides an excellent, competitive practice environment.

We all enjoy competing and playing games because they motivate us to better attention. However, do not get caught in the mind set that "official games" should be played. Create your own games which focus on stroke development first, and gradually introduce accuracy.

Jimmy Connors is perhaps the best example of the principle of speed before accuracy. Connors tells the story of how he lost many tournaments as a young player because he continued to stroke the ball well while his ten- to twelve-year-old opponents merely blooped it back. But eventually, his well-learned swings were controlled to produce some of the best strokes in the world.

GRADUATED STRESS FOR IMPROVED STROKES

As your tennis strokes become more consistent in practice, begin to add stressful situations. Change the homemade games you play so that they require a little more concentration. Force yourself to

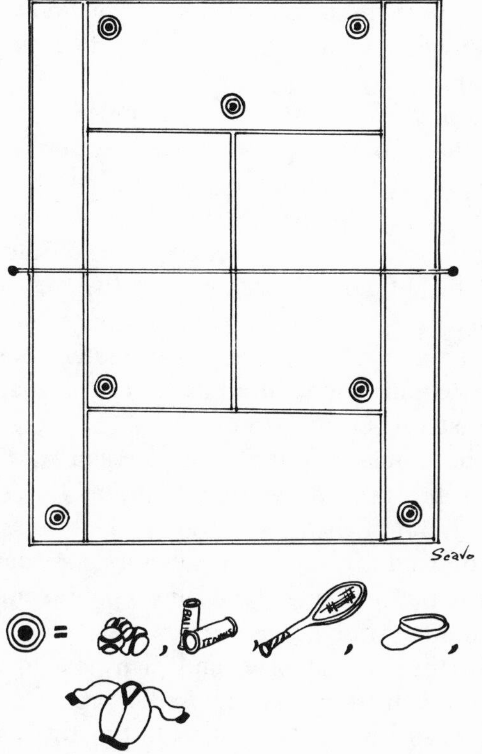

Targets placed on the court can lead to motivating practice.

take the net, to serve and volley, or to hit as many backhands as you can. After all, if you are not willing to try your best in practice, you will have difficulty executing in a match.

The major problem with adopting this philosophy is making the initial choice. Do you really want to become a better player? If so, you must consciously choose which strokes you will work on and decide how seriously you want to develop them. If you decide that a topspin backhand is an important skill to develop, and you have practiced it consistently, then force yourself into stressful situations and be sure to try it. It is awfully easy to fall back on your former, safe chip backhand—but if you are serious about a topspin backhand, then force yourself to use it.

The decision to use new skills in practice will make it much easier to execute them in competition. If you know that you can hit that backhand while playing hard in practice, then using it in the game will be easy.

When you arrive at the court to practice, get into your standard routine. Loosen up and do the flexibility exercises discussed earlier. Take a couple of deep, slow breaths and mentally go through your practice plan and goals. It is important at this time to imagine your planned practice paying off and helping you be successful. Do not allow any negative or self-defeating thoughts—such as "What am I doing out here while others are inside drinking and taking it easy?"—to enter your mind. You have made a commitment to attain a certain goal—stick with practice to reach it, be persistent.

From the moment your practice session starts to the moment it ends, be sure that you concentrate. Don't let yourself merely hit a hundred balls; slow down, analyze, and carefully practice the desired strokes. Do not allow a sloppy day of practice. It is too easy to pick up bad habits doing a sloppy practice session which may hinder your progress for weeks. Start learning and preparing for tournament play, and plan how to control your arousal level. If you are tired and bored in practice, learn how to get yourself up and ready. If you start hitting the ball poorly and you feel yourself getting anxious and distracted, practice controlling the focus of your attention. Get your confidence back, take a deep breath, relax, go through your routine, and hit.

Most tennis players who have put some thought into their game recognize that they may hit the ball slightly differently on certain days. Start to recognize these tendencies. What happens when you are tired? How about when you feel strong? As you learn to recognize these tendencies, experiment with correcting them. Know that you can self-correct them when they occur in a tournament.

As you start getting your strokes grooved, start to utilize the concept known as model training—start to simulate the competitive situation in your practice sessions. Begin to change strokes with each practice shot in a sequence similar to that likely to occur on the court. Practice cross-courts, down-the-lines, drop shots, topspins, sidespins, underspin shots, etc. Hit into the wind, with the wind, against cross winds. Instead of skipping practice on sunny, extremely bright days, dress for them, practice serving with the sun in your eyes, etc. Do the same on cold days. Study the flight of the ball in these various situations and record the information in your brain; record particularly important facts, in a little book you can always carry with you. Be sure you have also recorded in detail your practice goals. Do you tend to hit a low or high ball? How does the height and pace of your opponent's ball affect your strokes? It will help you when you are in an uncomfortable situation during competition.

Include anxiety and distractions in your practice sessions. Set up contests with an opponent. During the contest have your opponent make noises, make unexpected movements, make you feel self-conscious by describing how your serve looks as you are about to hit, etc. You'll be amazed at how well you can learn to serve or stroke despite these distractions.

As the competitive event draws near, it is best to emphasize confidence development in both your physical and mental practice. As mentioned previously, if you haven't mastered it by now, forget it until after the tournament. On the last two days of preparation, do everything possible to increase the likelihood of hitting only good shots. Spend extra time on building confidence in your serve and basic groundstrokes. Practice lots of deep, solid groundstrokes. Again, take your time and concentrate as you practice. Mentally imagine and feel only perfect shots. Visualize successful outcomes. Imagine arriving at the tournament, signing in, practicing and playing always with successful results. Do not allow anxieties or self-doubts to cross your mind.

Play the tournament and do your best—always go through your routine and control your attention as you know you should.

At the end of each match, analyze your mistakes or bad shots and mentally correct them. Before going to sleep visually imagine playing the match perfectly and go to sleep ready to do your best tomorrow.

Remember, concentration in a match is thinking in the present, not in the past or future. If you find yourself thinking about blowing the last overhead and being considered a "choker" or fearing that if you win you'll have more pressure to win again, recognize these thoughts as anxieties and distractions and induce relaxation. Work with positive imagery to calm your mind and to get the proper frame of mind back again.

SETTING YOUR GOALS AND ATTAINING THEM

The information presented so far can be of great value to you. It can also be of little or no value, for unless you were born an unbelieveably gifted tennis player, you need to set goals. You must also plan a strategy for attaining those goals, plan the program effectively, and then have the self-discipline and desire to practice regularly. The following program will help you be effective so you know you won't be wasting practice, and you will be motivated because you will be continually seeing your improvement.

There are at least six steps which are crucial to the goal-setting process. Ask yourself the following questions:

Step 1—Know yourself.

How good a tennis player am I now?

How good would I like to be?

Why in the past have I not progressed as I would like?

Am I self-disciplined?

Do I concentrate when I practice?

Am I willing to take responsibility for my achievement or would I rather blame others or luck for my success or failure?

Step 2—Know what you know.

What are the skills required for success in tennis?

Do I understand the various strokes and strategies and rules?

Do I understand the mental aspects of tennis?

Do I know the strength requirements necessary for good strokes?

Do I know which muscle groups must be relaxed to hit consistently?

Do I have enough flexibility to develop full rotation and power?

Step 3—Identify your strengths and weaknesses.

What are my greatest strengths as a tennis player?

What are my weaknesses as a tennis player?

Do I know how to go about improving each of them?

How much time am I willing to put into my practicing?

Do I tend to only practice the shots I enjoy?

Am I practicing perfectly to insure success or am I just putting in time?

Do I tend to practice my strengths, or the shots I am already good at and spend very little time on my weaknesses?

Is the amount of time I spend on each shot related not only to what needs the most improvement, but also the shots which mean the most to tennis success?

Step 4—Define goals.

Are my goals challenging, yet realistic?

If I put the time and effort planned into them, will I attain them?

Once I attain them, will I raise my level of aspiration and goals?

Step 5—Plan for goal attainment.

How will I practice to meet goals?

How much time do I have to attain my long-term goals?

How can I best use the resources at my disposal in the time I have to learn?

What will my plan of attack be for attaining each of my subgoals?

How much will I attain each day, week, month, year?

Step 6—Evaluate programs and reestablish goals.

How can I evaluate my progress?

Is my improvement on schedule?

If not, why not, and what changes am I going to make?

Do I have suitable equipment?

Do I have confidence in my instructor and strokes, or is a change needed?

STEPS IN GOAL SETTING

1. Know yourself.
2. Know what you know.
3. Identify your strengths and weaknesses.
4. Define goals.
5. Plan for goal attainment.
6. Evaluate progress and reestablish goals.

SAMPLE PROGRAM

Evaluate Where You Are at Present

Consistency and depth. Go to the practice court and hit 20 balls with each stroke while swinging smoothly. Compare your stroke to the ideal. Are you aiming too low over the net? Are you getting enough depth on your groundstrokes? Can you identify any problems? Establish a remedial program based on your goals and go to work.

Go back to practice, set up specific goals, such as hitting 20 consecutive forehand drives between the service line and the baseline. Start scheduling your practice. Be sure to go through the process with each stroke.

Plan for Attaining Your Goals

The following is a sample goal-setting program:

Goal: Hit 20 consecutive forehands between the service line and baseline

Major weakness: Poor swing plane and weight transfer on forehand side

Date: March 1

Present skill level: Can hit 9 forehands out of 20 between the service and baselines; tested on 3 consecutive days (record on appropriate date on calendar)

Long-term goal: To hit target area 20 times consecutively (record on calendar on June 1)

Assess Reasons for Inaccuracy

Set time schedule for short- and long-term goals.

Long-term goals: Accomplish by June 1

Improvement required: 11 shots better out of 20 attempted

Total practice days: 90

Time per day spent practicing forehand at present: 40 practice shots per day at miscellaneous points during practice session

Time per day planned next 90 days: Minimum of 60 forehands per day, hitting each shot while concentrating on target (record on calendar under "Planned")

Short-term goal: 12 consecutive forehands by April 1 (record on calendar for April 1)

You will be likely to experience rapid improvement at the lower skill level. As you get better it will slow down because there is less room for improvement as your skill level gets higher. Each day you practice record the number of balls hit or length of practice time. Every two weeks record your score on the test on three consecutive sequences. Record your best test score. If you are progressing ahead of schedule, raise your goal. If progressing too slowly, check to see if you are practicing correctly. Are you establishing a target? Do you need to devote more time to practicing your forehand?

Continue to Practice on Schedule

Each day record your amount of practice on this weakness on your calendar. Retest every two weeks and mark your score on your calendar. This serves as both a daily reminder that you are working on a goal, and a motivator by charting your improvement. Keep it on your desk, or in some prominent location.

Spend ten to fifteen minutes each day inducing relaxation, making a self-statement of your commitment to improving. Do not fail to allow yourself time for your mental training.

Develop a Positive Mental Set

An ideal time for inducing relaxation is just before going to sleep at night (unless you tend to fall asleep too quickly). Once you are relaxed, use external imagery to go through hitting your forehand. Next, practice internal imagery of hitting your forehand. Finally, and very importantly, visually imagine yourself going through tomorrow's planned practice session and recording your results on your calendar. Think positively about how good you will feel when you play well in June as a result of your efforts. If any self-doubts enter your mind, tell yourself, "stop," and utilize self-talk in a positive manner. Talk to yourself about the improvements that will result from perfect practice and planning for success.

9
Playing the Game

Becoming a success on the tennis court requires a wide range of physical and mental skills. There are several strategies that could greatly benefit your game from a psychological perspective.

Try at all times to play within your own abilities. Know which shots you can execute well and which shots not so well. Most of the time, try to control how safely or aggressively you play based on the likelihood of being rewarded. Usually an inclination to play safely rather than boldly will have the greater payoff in tennis. If you decide that you need to play aggressively, do so with a shot that you are likely to execute successfully. In other words, be aggressive when necessary, but don't gamble unreasonably.

Prior to serving the first ball be sure that you are ready and positive. Do not allow yourself to start out filled with fear of losing or looking bad. This approach can only cause you to play "tight" and defensively. Do not become a player who has to be behind in a match before getting started. Starting successfully will be a benefit to muscle and mind relaxation. It will aid your confidence and put the pressure on your opponent. Concentrate on returning every shot and going for winners only when the percentages are with you. But even when you go for winners, give yourself a couple of feet for error. Don't aim for the edge of the line.

ARE YOU READY TO PLAY COMPETITIVE TENNIS?

Organized competition can be a great way to test your tennis skills and your tennis competence. Match play is a good way to identify your strengths and weaknesses and improve your overall level of play. You will be able to test your own skills and learn to develop and try various strategies in a variety of competitive settings.

Challenges

Challenge ladders and pyramids provide a comfortable way to begin competitive tennis. Both challenge ladders and pyramids work on the concept that you may challenge anyone directly above you. The structure of "pyramids" generally provides for more than one person on the next level, therefore increasing the opportunities for competition. These structures provide *direct challenges* by allowing competition with players roughly equal to or slightly better than you. If you challenge someone above you and win, you move up to the next level of competition and your opponent moves down to your former slot. If you lose, you retain your previous position.

League Play

Playing as a representative of your local court group provides an opportunity to experience the pleasure and challenge of competition while simultaneously meeting players from other clubs or areas. The team aspect promotes both friendship and competition.

Tournaments

Single-elimination tournaments allow you to progress against opponents who are progressively more skilled. You must test your skills against someone else, and if you win, you progress to

Challenge ladders and pyramids provide good opportunities to test your skills.

the next stage. Ultimately the best two competitors face each other in the final match.

Consolation and double-elimination tournaments provide for competitive experience against a wider range of players. Consolation playing is provided for players who lose in the first round of an elimination type tournament. This provides for at least two matches for all players, even if they lose in the first round of the regular tournament.

Double-elimination tournaments allow for each player to continue to compete until they lose to two different opponents. This gives all players a chance to redeem themselves if they lose one match or have a "bad day."

Round-robin events provide a good opportunity to play many other people. For example, if there are eight entrants, you will play each of the other seven competitors. You play each of the other contestants at least once, and the winner is determined by the person with the best total record. This format guarantees that each player participates in a rather large number of matches, without respect to having won or lost.

PLAYING A MATCH

Match play requires not only good physical skills but also consistent and confident play. During a match this is particularly important during the first few games of each set. The initial play should be steady and confident. You should strive to get your first serve in and play each shot deep and to your opponent's weakness. Focus on good shots, without errors.

As the match progresses, you may wish to be more aggressive if things are going well. If things are not going well, go back to the basics. If your game begins to fall apart, it is time to rebuild your confidence. Take a little off your first serve and be sure to hit it deep. Focus on the "sure thing" and your most reliable strokes. As your match gets closer to completion and tighter in score, make sure that you concentrate on playing one point at a time. Avoid thinking about winning, losing, "blowing it," or "pulling off an upset." All these thoughts are distractors—they can destroy a game that is going well or further confuse a rapidly deteriorating game. You must play one point at a time and concentrate on the ball.

COACH YOURSELF

When on the tennis court, you are alone. Utilize what you know about the physical and mental side of playing tennis. Prepare yourself for success; monitor your arousal level; concentrate and avoid distractions, and be good to yourself. Treat your errors positively: record them mentally or ask a friend to write them down and then forget them while playing the match at hand. Correct them when it is time to practice.

Remember to breathe deeply and slowly. Slow your walking pace down as the tension level rises. If you feel you need to stop, bend down and tie your shoe even if you have to untie it first!

Learning to coach yourself also means learning to know yourself. You must be able to evaluate your own tennis abilities. Most importantly, learn to judge your own stress and tension

GAUGING STRESS LEVELS IN TENNIS

Instructions: Circle the response which most agrees with your response to the situation described next to it.

Situation	*Strongly Agree*	*Mildly Agree*	*Mildly Disagree*	*Strongly Disagree*
1. I can remain calm even when my partner shows up late for a match.	1	2	3	4
2. I get upset when our opponents talk between points or take too long between serves.	4	3	2	1
3. It bothers me to play with others who serve faster than I do, or who rush me on the court side change.	4	3	2	1
4. Players who spend a lot of time looking for a "lost ball" or one that rolled three courts down make me mad.	4	3	2	1
5. I get upset by players who never hit the ball directly back to me when I am serving.	4	3	2	1
6. I take my time between serves and do not double-fault.	1	2	3	4
7. I am self-conscious and/or uncomfortable when I play with players who are better than I am.	4	3	2	1
8. Players talking on the adjacent court do not bother me.	1	2	3	4
9. I often find myself hurrying between games to save time.	4	3	2	1
10. When I play with someone for the first time, I often feel tense and play poorly.	4	3	2	1

Maximum Score = 40   My Total Score ________

Zone	*Score*	*Tension Level*
A	40–36	Considerably above average
B	35–29	Above average
C	28–21	Average
D	20–14	Below average
E	13–10	Considerably below average

levels. Take a moment and respond to the questions posed on the following self-scoring test for gauging levels in tennis.

If your score of the stress self-test is average or above, you will benefit from learning to control your stress. The stressors of tennis are great, but you can learn to control your own response to stressful situations.

PLAYING DOUBLES

For the large number of club tennis players, a major percentage of their tournament experience has been playing in doubles tournaments. Without a doubt, psychological aspects of team play will be a major determinant of success or failure in such situations.

Many tennis players have carefully considered the strategy of selecting a partner. The most typical question asked is: Should I play with a partner with similar or very different skills and abilities? This is a very pertinent question.

A doubles team must be able to communicate, or their chances for success are diminished greatly. Some players seem to automatically communicate and develop into successful tennis teams. Many others, however, have all the prerequisite skills to be effective but never achieve success in team matches. For such teams success will only come from improved communication. Partners must communicate effectively and build rather than destroy each other's confidence.

Doubles partners must be compatible players whose strengths and weaknesses complement each other. You need not be the best of friends, but neither should you intimidate each other. Rather, you must harness your skills and energies and make them work for your team.

Partners must remember that each person's objective is to maximize the performance of the other. You must feed each other's self-confidence, since if one is in a slump, both players' morale is jeopardized. You must help your partner not feel an overwhelming sense of guilt over letting you down.

Self-Image Protection

If your partner is playing badly, it is essential that you continue to display confidence in her. Be careful not to detach yourself from your partner—you are a team and must support each other both verbally and nonverbally. You must bring out the best in each other. Focus on the good shots, remind each other of similar times when you have pulled through, etc.

Allow your partner to protect her self-image, but do not overpraise or patronize. A general rule in doubles might be the less talk the better. Chattering away may be tempting but distracting since it may alter the focus of attention. A word or two of encouragement is all that is needed.

Be Honest with Your Partner

Doubles players must be honest with their partners. Good doubles players, on either mixed or same-sex teams must feel confident and comfortable with each other and must be able to freely communicate. It is particularly important to be able to admit strengths and weaknesses.

Your doubles partner needs to know your relative ability and your preferences. What are your best and worst shots? Do you like to play the net? Poach? Hit overheads? Serve and volley? If you can be honest, you will have a much better chance of becoming a great team.

Don't let your ego (or your social self) get in the way. Many women feel uncomfortable discussing their great overheads or their terrible backhands. Men have the same problems—they hate to admit they'd rather hit a forehand or play lobs after they bounce. But if you can be honest and admit your relative skills, you can play as a *team.*

Doubles teams must talk to each other. You should try to be encouraging about your games, but avoid being overly sweet, especially if your partner's game is not doing well. The most useful communication may occur when you tell your partner what

To be a great team, discuss your strengths and weaknesses with each other.

you hope to do on the next point. Such conversations help your partner anticipate the play and take advantage of your plans.

Communication in doubles must be a two-way street. Under most circumstances, both players should help identify strategy and the team's strengths and weaknesses. This approach will help insure the most effective use of both players' skills.

Your doubles partner should be a team player. You must be able to rely on your partner to help you in victory and stand with you in defeat. The great doubles pairs in pro tennis, Stan Smith and Bob Lutz, Martina Navratilova and Billie Jean King, do not play flashy doubles, but rather concentrate on keeping the ball effectively in play and letting their opponents make the errors.

Your partner should have good all-around tennis skills. Similarly, your contribution to the team must be solid. For example, getting your first serve in is a key to good doubles play. You should focus on hitting a solid, deep first serve in order to help your team remain in control. Another option for improved team play is to hit most serves down the middle of the court so that the return will come back to you or your partner.

Communicating with Your Partner

Open communication is crucial for successful doubles play. It is important that you and your partner be honest with each other. Be as open as possible about your relative strengths and weaknesses.

Good communication requires complete openness. The greater the amount of information shared by you and your partner, the better chance for successful team play. For example, consider what two experts in group dynamics, Luft and Ingham, suggest in terms of awareness. Their model, the Johari Window,* which can be very helpful to the doubles team, can be viewed as having four separate parts. Part A, the area of free activity, or open area, refers to behavior and motivation known to yourself and known to others. In a new team, this openness is very small. There may not be much free and spontaneous interaction. As the team remains intact for extended periods of time, this openness

The Johari Window.

	Known to Self	Unknown to Self
Known Partner	A Open and Free	B Blind
Unknown to Partner	Hidden or Avoided C	Unknown D

*J. Luft and H. Ingham. *The Johari Window: A Graphic Model of Interpersonal Awareness.* Proceedings of the Western Training Laboratory in Group Development (Los Angeles: University of California, Extension Office, August, 1955).

grows larger, and in general both partners are apt to be free to be more like themselves and perceive others as they really are. Part B, the blind area, is where others can see things in ourselves of which we are unaware. Part B may shrink in size very slowly because there may be "good" reasons of a psychological nature to blind ourselves to certain things we feel or do. The avoided or hidden area (part C) represents things we know about ourselves but fail to reveal to others (often weaknesses or skills about which we feel sensitive). These hidden strengths and weaknesses are reduced in size and number as we become more and more open with our partners. As an atmosphere of mutual trust is developed there is less need to hide pertinent thoughts or feelings. The final area, the area of unknown activity (part D), points to the area where neither you nor others are aware of certain behaviors or motives.

A basic goal for every doubles team should be to increase the area of free and open communication (A) and reduce the unknown areas (B, C, and D). Be honest with your partner. The likelihood of much greater use of the knowledge and skills of both partners will be increased with greater openness. Opinions and ideas will be communicated more often, and less time will be spent on self-defensive and ego-involving behaviors which are likely to hinder tennis performance.

Improving Communication

In the early stages of team formation both partners may think and feel in an independent manner. In other words, each member will tend to rely on his own feelings, impressions, and judgments as a guide to behavior. There will be times when independent action will be required, but an important quality of the mature team is interdependence of members.

Tennis players who wish to improve the communication in their teams must be willing to open themselves to their partners. Communication will not change if this doesn't happen. Both players must be willing to be flexible and open.

The following are questions doubles partners can use to

increase their cohesiveness and performance efficiency. Both partners must make a commitment to being as open and honest as possible if they truly wish to benefit to the fullest:

1. What are your greatest strengths as a tennis player? What are your best shots? Are you a fast or slow starter? Do you recover from trouble well? Are you steady? Are you a great scrambler? Do you like to put the ball away and end points effectively? Do you play your best in the clutch?

2. What are your major weaknesses as a tennis player? What are your poorest shots? If you start slowly, are you in trouble? Are you inconsistent? Are you a poor server? Are you weak on high backhands?

3. When do you play with the most confidence? Do you like to serve first? Do you get better when playing with a lead?

4. When do you get the most anxious? Do you feel a lot of stress that hurts you in the early games? Do you fall apart if your partner is having a poor day? Do you usually have trouble on the closing points?

5. Which behaviors by a partner tend to help you play better? Do you need to be positively encouraged? Do you need to feel that you are contributing to the team? Do you need to talk over strategy a lot? Do you prefer not to talk much?

Be sure to discuss your answers to these questions with your partner. In addition, let your answers to these questions guide your own practices.

Beyond Communication

Clearly, interdependence is important to team success. This does not mean, however, that you should not take personal responsibility for your team's success or failure. Recognize that you are at least one-half the team and that how you perform will be crucial.

Do not allow yourself to become the kind of partner who takes responsibility for the match outcome when you win, but blames failure on your partner. Making negative comments about your partner's performance can be devastating to your team. Making negative comments about your own play following a match will not hurt your team. But making negative statements about your partner's performance to other tennis players can be retold to your partner and hinder your future success.

Try at all times to encourage and help your partner to play better. Listen to your partner when he speaks to you on the court. Show your interest and respect. Prevent at all times negative emotional behaviors from hindering your play.

Dealing with Errors

All tennis players make errors, but good players correct those errors in their minds and remember the good shots.

Do not apologize for errors, either to yourself or to your partner. Apologies only focus attention on the error. Instead, you must imagine the better shot and put the error out of your mind. Remember that winners see what they want to happen, while losers replay what they fear might happen.

Apologizing for errors may also be detrimental to your own confidence while it builds confidence in your opponents. Seeing you worry about past errors or weaknesses may give your opponents the edge by boosting their morale. In doubles, this is even more critical since your apologies not only reinforce your opponents, but may confirm to your partner the fact that you are making a lot of mistakes.

Recognize when you can help your partner and when your helpful advice is of little value. The best way to assess this situation is to try to view the situation from your partner's perspective rather than from your own. Often they differ markedly. If your partner is playing great when you talk, keep your comments positive but general. For instance, if your partner is serving well, don't start constantly saying, "Hey, you're really serving well. The ball is really flying off your racket." Such statements will only sensitize your partner. They may also encourage conscious rather than subconscious performance.

If, on the other hand, your partner is playing poorly, do everything you can to take the pressure off and build confidence. Behave as though your partner's play is not bothering you. Don't try to become your partner's coach. He can probably work out of his problems faster without your constant advice—especially if you are in the middle of a critical match. On the other hand, if you decide that improvement is the goal for this match, this may be a good time to help. In either case, the first time your partner makes a good swing or shot use it as an opportunity to build confidence. Perhaps the best thing you can do to help your partner's confidence is to continue playing your own solid game when your partner is struggling.

Should You Overule a Line Call by Your Partner?

One of the most difficult calls in tennis occurs when your partner has called a ball "out" and you believe it is "in." Should you (1) call it "good"? (2) ask for a "let"? or (3) say nothing, thereby supporting your partner's call which you believe is wrong?

Partners must both protect and trust each other. If you

OUT?

believe the ball was "good," you should be intent on ruling in that fashion. But to save the positive interaction of a good doubles team, tell your partner and let him change the call or make the final decision.

PLAYING MIXED DOUBLES

Mixed doubles can be great for developing your game. It can put you in situations that will force growth and improvement. If you are the weaker player, you will have to hit overheads, volleys, deep lobs, and return exceptionally fast-paced serves.

Mixed doubles should be fun. You should learn from playing it. When you play mixed doubles does your partner have you stand in the alley and hit five shots per set? Do you happily oblige? If you do, realize that your game is headed nowhere but downhill.

If you allow yourself to be dominated, *stop*. Be assertive, speak up for yourself. Tell your partner that you want to play your half of the court and learn how to play doubles better. However, if your net game and your overhead are not well developed, then be honest. Admit it to your partner and commit yourself to improvement. Until you improve tell your partner that in practice matches you will play your half of the court so you can improve. In tournaments you will stay to the side until your game is ready. But you decide when that is. When you are ready you will cover your half of the court. You will hit your own overheads.

Explain to your doubles partner that if he really is competitive and wants to win, then he should get out with you and help you develop your overhead. Complaining and hogging your half of the court will not help.

When Husbands and Wives (or Friends) Play

It is difficult to play with those you love. But it is not impossible. Look at playing with your husband or wife on the court as an exciting challenge.

One of the major problems commonly confronted by husband-and-wife teams is a difference in competitiveness. Often one person, frequently the male, is very competitive and plays to win. Some women may play just to have some recreation time with their husbands. They love having everyone see them on the court together. They care little about winning or losing. Of course, this situation can also be reversed.

If you decide to continue to play, you will have your work cut out for you. You will have to try to understand the other person's perspective. Many people, especially men, have been taught that they should always be competitive. On the other hand, many women believe friendship is more important than winning.

Both types must learn to do their best. If your team's best is not enough, it is OK. The key is you have tried. If you wish to do better, you both must work at improving your skills. Half the fun is in learning to improve both your games. If you will be open and honest with each other and drill each other, husband-and-wife doubles can be a source of joy. But if one partner practices and works to improve and the other does nothing, frustration will indeed persist.

RULE 1 IN DOUBLES: HIT AT THE WEAKER PLAYER

A key advantage in doubles is to hit at the weaker partner—so when they hit nine out of ten shots at you, they are telling you something. Don't get upset. Do not respond emotionally. Keep your composure and decide to enjoy the situation. This is your golden opportunity. You are going to get to hit more shots than anyone else. This will be great for your game. If you can concentrate and remain patient, you will win a lot of matches. The more times you hit the ball back, the more likely that some opponent will overhit and miss a shot before you do.

Too many players respond emotionally when they are the weaker partner. Do you believe it is cruel and inhuman, or that you are being picked on if the opposition hits the ball to you? If so, your self-defeating attitude may prevent rather than increase growth in your game.

10

Preparing for a Match

PREMATCH PREPARATION: THE FIRST STEP TO IMPROVING CONCENTRATION AND INTENSITY

Your prematch preparation presets your mind to concentrate during the upcoming match. The concentration and intensity displayed by top-level players is not something magical. Likewise, despite many popular misconceptions, these are not qualities that you are born with or without. Concentration and intensity can be learned and improved upon. The relaxation-training exercises and concentration-improvement techniques outlined in this book will help greatly. But alone they will not do the entire job. They must be combined with an effective approach to prematch preparation.

There are two very important attentional factors which distinguish the average player from the top-level player. First, the better players spend a much greater percentage of their time thinking about the upcoming tennis match in a productive manner. Do not allow yourself to overlook the importance of this point. It is an important step in preparing the mind for what is to come. Second, better players recover from their mistakes and failures more readily. Take notice! *Better players also make mis-*

takes and have failures. But they don't let them destroy their performance. They have learned the importance of getting their minds back to the task at hand during the intensity of competition. Again, the ability to effectively manage the destructive tendencies of these pressure-filled situations begins in your prematch preparation.

You must learn to emulate the approach to preparation used by the pros and some of the better players that you will compete against. Even if your strokes aren't as well developed as the pros', there is no reason for you not to think and concentrate as they do. Your mental preparation can overcome many mechanical and physical liabilities. Certainly Bjorn Borg has what might be considered mechanical weaknesses in his strokes, and Tracy Austin is not the quickest athlete on the women's tour. But both these players have maximized their performance by a great mental approach to the sport. You, too, must maximize the mental advantage that you can possess if you want to.

Your mental preparation begins by analyzing the skills and abilities of your upcoming opponent. Physical and mental qualities must be included here. Once established, compare these abilities to your own in a *realistic* manner. Decide how you can use your unique skills to advantage in capitalizing on your opponent's weaknesses. Do not try to fool yourself. Devise a strategy that you will be able to execute. Next, try to predict your opponent's response to your strategy. How can you take advantage of your opponent's anticipated response to your playing style? Vividly imagine the upcoming match and specific situations in your mind. Be prepared for anything.

Where is your game likely to break down if it's going to? How can you prevent this from happening? A good way to formulate this part of your pregame strategy is to pretend that you are your opponent and are preparing to play yourself. How would you play yourself? In using this approach remember that you must view your game from the other person's perspective. Perhaps you have no confidence in your backhand approach shot despite frequently hitting winners. Your opponent may only recall the winners and try to avoid your backhand.

However, it is equally important not to avoid your weaknesses. Your opponent probably knows what they are. Anticipate that your opponent will try to take advantage of them. Take your time and develop a sound, rational strategy for defeating your opponent. Carefully analyze your strategy. Check it for flaws and then accept it and stop analyzing it. Make a decision, believe in it, and stick with it. Go over and over your strategy in your mind until it is a part of you. Believe in it and don't second-guess yourself. Decide if you will stay with this strategy for the entire match or only part of it.

You must, however, be careful not to let your game plan become so mechanized that it is inflexible. If you ever wish to attain your potential you must at all times remain willing to change. You must be confident, relaxed, and emotionally controlled in order to make effective adjustments from your prematch plan. With experience and mental control this will become easier to do.

What will you do if your plan doesn't work? Will you stay with it or change? If you change your strategy, when will you change and to what will you change? You must make these decisions ahead of time. You can't afford to let yourself think about making these decisions for the first time when you are extremely nervous and down 6–2, 4–1 in the match. Your mind will most likely not work very effectively if you have not planned ahead. Chances are that you will choose an ineffective strategy and further dampen your chances for success.

Does all this appear to you to be a lot of work and perhaps unenjoyable? To highly motivated players this is fun. It is a crucial part of the success they so desire. The tougher the opponent they must play, the more time and thought they put into prematch preparation. Occasionally, even the best players overlook an opponent and fail to prepare effectively and get beat. This is a frequent cause of early-round upsets in tournaments. Consistent winners learn that they cannot make the mistake of overlooking mental preparation. This means that for most players whose physical skills are not that much better than their upcoming opponents, mental preparation will be even more crucial for each and every match. Be sure you give it the attention it deserves.

Many athletes who have fallen in love with the challenge of tennis have not had a background of structured sport experiences in which the importance of strategy was emphasized. If this applies to you, you may have difficulty understanding the importance of strategy. However, if you will give time and attention to it, you may realize that it can be fun to think about and talk about strategy.

You would do well to take a lesson from some of the "Super Senior Tennis Players" around the country. Watch them closely and observe the emphasis that they place on strategy. Two of our favorites—seventy-year-old Alphonso Smith, the only person ever to win U.S. singles championships fifty years apart, (both as a junior and as a super senior) and fifty-five-year-old Charlotte Lee, a national platform doubles champion and a great tennis player—have learned that they can beat many youngsters by making the maximum use of strategy. They have recognized that a well-thought-out game plan can overcome a loss of foot speed, pace, or a big serve. It can help you also.

Some players who are highly motivated to be successful tournament champions have found another solution to the amount of time and thought that must be given to strategy: they have hired a coach. They have faith that their coach knows their game well enough to plan their workouts and match strategy. This approach gives the young player more time to relax, practice strokes, and do schoolwork. It can be very effective. But it does have its drawbacks. It can be very expensive and hard to find a dedicated knowledgeable coach. It might be harder yet to find one that you will believe in. Without a completely trusting player-coach relationship, you are probably better off by yourself. A talented coach can perceive more subtle weaknesses in your opponent and devise a strategy for more advanced play than you may be capable of designing. If you are motivated enough and can afford a coach, it may be to your advantage to hire one. Be sure to take your time and be selective.

FEARS THAT DISTRACT

Players at different ages tend to have different fears that may hinder their concentration. In the younger years (of age or tennis experience) players tend to fear that they won't make it. They worry that they will never be very successful. Much effort is dedicated to proving to themselves, their parents, spouses, and friends that they can be good.

As you become successful you may begin to fear losing skills or being beaten by someone younger. Eventually fears revolve around getting too old to continue winning—the fear that you won't be remembered. Most everyone has had these fears. They are quite normal. Be sure that you don't waste valuable practice time worrying about what might happen.

THE TWENTY-FOUR HOURS BEFORE A MATCH

You can start to focus your concentration a bit more intensely as the match you have been awaiting grows closer. Your goal is obviously to channel your attention so that it peaks at match time.

Establish a Routine

Often players feel that a consistent *routine* for practice, sleep, food, preparing their equipment, and getting up in the morning is crucial to their success. This is particularly true of athletes who are consistently able to be mentally ready to perform at or near their peaks. If you haven't yet tried a specific routine for a fairly lengthy time period, give it a try. A comfortable routine will give you confidence and improve your concentration.

Despite the fact that a routine can give you consistency, there is one major drawback to putting too much emphasis on a set routine. The problem occurs when something unexpected happens which prevents you from following your routine. It may be a flat tire on the way to a tournament, a ride that doesn't show up, or an extremely short or extended match just prior to yours. Whatever the cause, you must be certain that dependence on your routine doesn't prevent you from playing well under these circumstances. As a preventive measure it is an excellent idea to occasionally play practice matches without your routine. This will help you recognize that you can play effectively without a routine. The routine is only designed to give you *more* confidence and help you feel comfortable. Don't let it become your enemy. Similarly, if you are uncomfortable utilizing a routine at all, do not feel ineffective. A good routine is merely an individualized attempt at gaining control over your thoughts, strategy, and confidence.

When you go out to practice the day before a tournament match, have a specific practice plan designed ahead of time and stick with it. Try to have your practice partner hit the shots you need to practice. Try to build confidence in your practice session. Do not let negative thoughts destroy your practice. If your timing is a little off, slow down until you get it back, and don't start worrying that you've lost it. You haven't. You're just a little tight, and that will go away as you get into the match tomorrow.

Try to keep your practice shorter and less strenuous than normal. Don't make the anxious mistake of overdoing it at the last moment.

Go home, try to relax, and have a good meal, preferably something with carbohydrates and without too much acid. Take your time and eat slowly. Go to bed at your normal time unless you must get up earlier than normal. Attempt to keep everything as close to normal as possible. Get up in the morning and have what you normally have for breakfast or opt for food high in carbohydrates, whichever you prefer.

Leave and get to the court well in advance of the starting time of your match. Do not let anything happen that will cause you increased tension or worry. You don't need it today.

THE PREMATCH WARM-UP

The warm-up for a match often determines the outcome of the match. How often have you won or lost a match during the warm-up? Probably more than once.

Coaches in team sports in particular have long understood

the important functions of warm-up. It is most certainly not a useless waste of time. The warm-up has many purposes, including (1) getting your body stretched out and warmed up, (2) getting the feel of your strokes, (3) evaluating the strengths and weaknesses of your opponent, and (4) gaining psychological control of your opponent.

The fourth purpose does not need to be a regular function of your warm-up. You will only need to use the warm-up in this manner when you are playing an important tournament match. If you were to use psychological ploys on a daily basis with your friends in casual matches you may soon have no opponents to play! You must carefully decide against which opponents you should and need to use the warm-up to gain a psychological advantage.

Psych-outs

Jimmy Connors once commented on the psych-outs and tantrums of opponents, specifically those of John McEnroe: "You can't let it get to you because . . . sometimes he plays better when he's steamed. Pancho Gonzalez used crowds and linesmen in his favor. I used to hang out with him, and it rubbed off. When I was younger, the more fits I threw the better I was. Now I save my energy for the important things."*

Psych-outs in tennis may take two different forms. You can use them to your own advantage by employing them against an opponent, or you may inadvertently use them against yourself by worrying too much about the other person, how you look, or what others are feeling about you and your tennis game. The accompanying table illustrates psych-outs used in warm-up that can work both ways.

If you determine that you must gain psychological control in the warm-up, you must plan a strategy ahead of time and then implement it. There are many ways to get into your opponent's head. As they are presented below, make certain that you under-

**Tennis*, April 1980, p. 14.

WARM-UP PSYCH-OUTS

Positive psych-outs—behavior that can help you gain an advantage for yourself	*Negative psych-outs* (confidence-reducing for yourself and confidence-building for your opponent)—behavior that can negatively affect you
Hitting all lobs deep and to backhand Teaching your opponent—correcting some aspect of his or her game Hitting only to an opponent's weaknesses Hitting your opponent's practice serve back for winners Returning all your opponent's overheads deep and occasionally for winners Comments such as: "No matter what anyone else says, your volley's pretty good—even if it's a little short." "Can't you hit me some groundstrokes with pace?" "Well, I'll do the best I can, but I have a bad back today." "I'm really tired, but I'll do the best I can." "Courts are sure in terrible shape." "Sure is too hot to play today—what are we doing here anyway?" "Aren't those people on the next court noisy—they will bother us all day."	Practice hitting real short to help opponent Worrying about getting the ball where your opponent can hit it Worrying that your shots will not allow opponent to practice volley Comments such as: "Would you like me to hit any special shot for you?" "I'm so glad we are finally getting to play—we must make sure that we get together some other time." "I don't know what I'm doing here—I feel like a klutz out here."

stand how and why they work so that you can immunize yourself against similar attempts by your opponents. Most of these psych-outs will attempt to get your opponent to respond emotionally to you. The result will be distraction and loss of concentration. Constantly search for factors that can help you. Many seemingly unimportant influences work for or against you. The way you dress, walk, and look at the person when you introduce yourself can all affect an opponent's response.

One approach used by many veteran players is to casually show up late for a match. They will never show up so late that they will have to default. They will, however, try to convey the message that they really are not taking you too seriously. The hope is that you will respond emotionally or try so hard that you fail. You may also be left standing in awe of this seasoned veteran. "How can I ever hope to beat players who are so confident that they can show up late for a match?"

Rosie Casals tells of the proficiency of her good friend, Billie Jean King. Once Rosie was leading 4–0 in the second set of a match when Billie Jean walked over, threw down her racket, and asked Rosie if she could borrow one of her spares. It was as if Billie Jean were saying, "My problem must be the racket—I'm the one who should be winning."

Billie Jean King's positive and strong personality has been a continuing asset to her. She was even too strong for the master of psych-outs, Bobby Riggs. In their famous Battle of the Sexes, Billie Jean was just too confident and disciplined to be susceptible to the simple psych-outs attempted by Riggs.

There are many pros at the psych-out game, including Gardner Malloy, Virginia Wade, and John McEnroe. Some are also masters at counteracting attempted psych-outs. Certainly, Chris Evert Lloyd, Tracy Austin, and Bjorn Borg have this talent. These players usually let nothing bother them. Of course, this itself can end up psyching out their opponents. After all, how do you beat anyone that good and that cool?

Indeed, psych-outs can often be quite subtle. For example, if your opponent is serving well, you might try commenting: "I've never seen you serve like this before. You sure are coming over the ball nicely." Your opponent may suddenly become conscious of her serve and start overanalyzing it and fall apart.

Conversely, the more you get lost in emotional response and think about your opposition, the less attention you are able to give to your own performance. For this reason the best advice is to go out and play your own game and warm up the way that you want to.

Do you meow or roar?

In general, if someone is wasting his time trying to psych you out, it's probably because he is not as confident as he would like to appear. But sometimes it is also due to his perception that you *can* be psyched out. So the more you avoid letting such attempts affect you, the more likely it is that they won't be used against you.

When psych-outs are used against you, be ready to combat them. If you like pace and rhythm, someday someone will give you nothing but junk to hit in warm-up. Someone else will go out and hit winners everywhere. When you come in to net to volley or hit overheads someone will hit lobs one foot inside the baseline. You name it and somebody will try it. Have you ever experienced such attempts being tried against you in the past? If so, how have you responded? Get to know yourself by studying how you *do* tend to respond. It will be the first step to improvement.

Avoiding (or Using) Psych-Outs

More matches have been won or lost as a result of psych-outs than most of us care to imagine. Their power to influence performance is indeed scary. How is it, then, that most tennis players know so little about them or how to prevent them from destroying their performance?

Psych-outs are always directed at another person's emotions. If they were received and responded to at an intellectual level, they would not be effective.

When opponents try to psych you out, no matter if it is before, during, or following a match, they will have one goal in mind. They will attempt to get you to become overly concerned with what other people think of you.

If you are so self-confident and content with yourself that you are totally unconcerned with yourself, psych-outs will not work against you. But if you are like most people, you *do* care to some extent what others think of you. Your perception of yourself is to some degree based upon the view that others have of you.

If you begin to believe that who you are and what people think of you are determined by how well you play tennis, you are a ready victim for a psych-out. Have you ever found yourself thinking, "She'll never play with me again, I'm so terrible," "I bet others are laughing at me," "Gosh, I'd like to impress them so that they would like me." If your answer to any of these is yes, then you have been psyched out. You have responded emotionally rather than intellectually. You have been distracted.

Psych-outs can be totally caused by you and your perception of others. But they may also be intentionally or unintentionally directed at you through another's words. You must be careful that you do not interpret unintentional psych-outs as intentional. A true friend may compliment your play with, "Great volley" or "I sure wish I had that shot" with the full intention of building your confidence. Don't perceive inaccurately that it was said for other reasons.

Regardless of how a message is intended, it can only psych you out if you let it. The first key to managing yourself is to realize that you are beginning to respond emotionally. Think "stop," walk away from play for a moment and "let go." Gain confidence from (1) the fact that you stayed in control in spite of the psych-out attempt and (2) the realization that you must have the edge if your opponent perceives the need to try to win by psyching you out. In effect, your opponent is saying, "I can't beat you with my physical skills alone, so I'm going to try to win the battle of the mind and the emotions." Fantastic: you have your opponent right where you want her, distracted and thinking about you. Now your job is to stay under control, play your shots one at a time, and concentrate on the ball. For now you have the psychological edge. Your opponent has managed to psych out only herself.

Remember to try to recognize psych-outs and respond to them intellectually rather than emotionally. Strive to be happy with who you are and what you are about. Have the desire to improve, but accept and be happy with who you are. People who base their feelings about you on your relative ability to hit a tennis ball are people you can do without.

Much has been written in recent years about how to psych out your opposition. You will be much better off if you apply the positive approach utilized in this book and do everything possible to perform up to your own ability. Simply recognize that reacting to any environmental situation on an emotional rather than an intellectual level will be detrimental to your game. When confronted with such situations, induce relaxation and respond in a rational manner.

Once you understand your opponent's attempts and gain self-awareness, how do you combat psych-outs? To begin with, expect these things to happen and be prepared to stay calm. If you need to, find a wall or a friend to hit with until you feel comfortable before you step on the court with your scheduled opponent.

You can further learn to combat psych-outs by employing *simulated* psych-out attempts in your practice sessions. Try playing a match with no on-the-court warm-up. Play a practice match where you never hit more than two shots in a row for the first four games. If you really wish to gain control of your mind, try playing a practice match where you purposely miss your first six overheads, volleys, and/or groundstrokes. On another day try flubbing all your warm-up serves. (See the accompanying "Mind Games.") The sooner you realize through understanding and guided practice that you can combat any of these situations if you control your emotions and focus all your thoughts on the ball, the better off you will be in combating attempted psych-outs during warm-ups.

MIND GAMES FOR PSYCH-OUT IMMUNIZATION

Play a practice match without any on-the-court warm-up.

Play a practice match with a maximum warm-up of two minutes.

Play a practice match in which you never hit more than two consecutive groundstrokes in the first four games.

Play a practice match after purposely flubbing every overhead or serve in warm-up.

Play a practice match after a warm-up in which you purposely hit every volley into the net.

Play a practice match in which you change rackets every game you play.

Play back-to-back sets on different court surfaces with no chance to warm up as you change courts.

Play a practice match while someone unexpectedly rolls balls across the court.

Play a practice match while someone on the sidelines is yelling personal statements about your or your game.

There is one other approach that you may wish to take in order to combat attempted psych-outs during warm-ups. You may need to be *assertive* if your opponent appears to be uncooperative. Call your opponent to the net and tell her the kind of shots that you want in warm-up and suggest that you don't intend to start play until you get them. If you would find this extremely difficult to do, you are probably a very nice person who cares about others. You may also be a little shy. We applaud you. Society needs more people like you. But on the tennis court, in a competitive tournament, you must sometimes learn to take care of what is rightfully yours. If you don't, you will be taken advantage of, and all your hours of practice will have been wasted.

We are not suggesting that you must be assertive and self-centered all the time. But you must be capable of being so in a tournament, against someone who is going to defeat you if you aren't. So if you want to play and do your best in tournaments, start getting ready for them. Learn to protect your rights and develop a strong will. If you don't, you will find other assertive players to be repulsive and impolite rather than strong-willed. If winning is not that important to you, fine. Accept it, and be happy with the level of competition that you enjoy.

The ideas that we have suggested are not as scary as they at first sound. If you try them enough, you will grow to love them and believe in your mental control no matter what happens to you. Take your time and try to understand these ideas one at a time. You will find that your warm-up will help you feel confident to play and that your concentration during play is improved.

THE MATCH IS ABOUT TO BEGIN

On match day don't let anyone or anything interfere with your preparation. Make sure ahead of time that you have all the equipment you will need, from shoelaces to sweatbands, to tissues, to rackets. Make sure you get to the court with plenty of time before the start of play. If you need to say hello to all your friends, do so early. Be sure that you give yourself enough time (at least thirty to sixty minutes) to spend by yourself to completely focus all your thoughts on the execution of your strategy. Block anything else out of your mind. Feel and picture yourself executing your strategy.

The second attentional factor that is crucial to success is the ability to recover quickly from errors or mistakes and get your mind back under control. This skill will be greatly enhanced if your prematch preparation includes anticipating every situation or distraction that could occur during the upcoming match. Anticipate how these situations are likely to influence your concentration and prepare yourself to recognize the distractions and get your mind back on the appropriate task. For example, if you are to play on a windy day, anticipate that the wind may cause you to miss some shots that you would normally make. This is in turn likely to cause you to get mad at the wind or yourself. As a result you may start thinking of the wind instead of the ball and miss more overheads. Decide that you will be ready if this starts to happen. You will stop the distracting thoughts and get your mind thinking "ball" or "stroke" rather than "wind."

There are many other situations that are likely to cause similar kinds of distractions. Environmental factors such as the sun, humidity, heat, cold, court surface, bad bounces, let calls, opponents that you love or dislike, bad calls, fear of hitting an opponent with an overhead, excitement over beating an opponent for the first time, or starting out expecting to lose can all cause you to become distracted.

Any of these problems can cause you to lose your confidence, remain distracted, and lose concentration for an extended time period if you let them. Try to anticipate certain situations that might bother you. Recognize that it is normal to have them cause you to make a mistake now and then. You are, after all, only human. The key is not to let them control your mind and destroy you for an extended length of time.

WHEN YOU FIND YOURSELF BEHIND—WHAT THEN?

There is probably no doubt about the fact that falling behind can make you more susceptible to distractions. Anyone can concentrate while hitting well and winning. But it's not so easy when you're behind. Your mind must be tough enough to prevent the excuses from dominating your attention. Often the mind will search for a justifiable excuse for failure which will protect your ego. You must not let such thoughts control your mind until the match has ended.

It is so easy to decide that today is not your day, that you're not good enough, or that you are too tired to continue giving your all. Do you ever remember being too tired when you were winning? How often have you ever been distracted by pain or injury when you were winning? Probably not very often. Pain and injuries are much more likely to be imagined when players are looking for excuses. Often, once you accept such thoughts and use them as an excuse, you will keep thinking about them and your play will get worse and worse because you are not concentrating effectively.

Anticipate that this is likely to occur when you are having a bad day. Take a moment to decide if you really are injured. If you are, establish whether or not your injury could lead to further damage to your body. If it can, stop playing. If it isn't going to hurt you to continue, block out the pain and focus all your attention on the ball and play tennis. There is no sense in playing with an excuse on your mind.

If after the match you realize that you did have an injury or you were out of shape, take care of the injury. When you continue practicing pick up your training and get into better shape. Don't ever let the same problem interfere with your performance again if you can help it.

LEARNING TO CONCENTRATE: BLOCK OUT OTHER INTERESTS

As you are probably beginning to realize, playing tennis up to your potential will require your time and attention. But certainly you will and should have other interests. You do not need to become a one-dimensional person. So you must learn when to concentrate and think only of tennis and when to think of your work, studies, family, or friends. Allowing yourself to think or worry about one thing while participating in the other will not help you find success or happiness.

It doesn't really matter how old you are. There will always be something or someone else trying to distract your attention from tennis. For the younger player, schoolwork and the demands of teachers, parents, and peers will cause problems as you aspire for success. Unfortunately, the easiest solution is to forget about your friends, schoolwork, or others and think only of tennis. But a much better solution is to accept the challenge of learning how to concentrate on one thing at a time. When you're at work or school, or doing work at home, concentrate on your work and nothing else. When you're practicing or playing tennis, do not allow yourself to worry about an upcoming meeting, test, or assignment. Discipline yourself to plan your time effectively and both your work and your tennis will benefit from it. The ability to concentrate is a skill that you will use throughout life.

Many players with family or work responsibilities constantly use a problem at home or on the job as an excuse for their inability to play up to their expectations. An excellent way to manage this challenge is to completely stop thinking of your job or homework when you get in the car to go play or practice. Get in the car and take a couple of deep, slow breaths and relax. As you drive or ride to the court, think only of tennis. Think through each part of your game. If you are going to practice, organize your practice session in your head and think about the shots on which you especially wish to work. If you have a match lined up, start planning your strategy. Continue this process while getting changed into your tennis clothes. As other thoughts enter your mind tell yourself "stop." Remind yourself that now is your tennis time. Any problem at work you will take care of later. If there is something important related to your job, school, or family that you are afraid you will forget, stop for a moment and write it down, and then get back to tennis. Do not give yourself excuses which will justify your lack of concentration when you play tennis.

11

Playing Better Tennis and Enjoying It More

DON'T FEEL GUILTY—YOU DESERVE A BREAK

There is a tendency for many people to believe that life is supposed to be all work and no play. You should either be at work or at home. You should be responsible. To some degree these feelings are valuable. They may help you justify your importance. They remind you that others need and depend on you. These feelings are important. How awful life would be if no one needed or depended upon you.

But sometimes we let these feelings get out of hand and they start to control us and cause problems. You take a break from work at noontime to play and you feel guilty that you aren't at work despite the fact that you frequently come in early, go home late, and work weekends. You go to play on a summer morning and you feel guilty that you're playing while your spouse is working. Especially when the local joker states: "It must be nice to just play all day while the rest of the world works for a living." Such remarks may make you feel so guilt-ridden that you turn down matches and stay away from tennis because you fear that people think that you are playing too much. Perhaps you have children

Tennis can be important to each individual.

and feel guilty whenever you leave them with a babysitter or alone while you play tennis. Many parents feel this way even though the greater part of their life is tirelessly devoted to their children.

Recognize that you do deserve the chance to get out and exercise and play. As a matter of fact, if you really love your work, your family and friends, and yourself, you *must* get out and *exercise.* It will be important to your mental and physical well-being and help make you a happier and more efficient person. So when you decide to play, forget about feeling guilty. Relax and enjoy playing. If your thoughts occasionally slip back to your work or home, don't feel bad. Everyone's do sometimes. But try to stop them and think about playing tennis, improving your game, and enjoying yourself and your opponent.

THIS IS YOUR TIME

An emotional encounter with a loved one, no matter if it's a parent, spouse, or lover, can also really influence your ability to concentrate on a given day. For this reason it helps if these intimate persons in a player's life realize that they can often significantly influence performance on the day of a pressure-filled match. Whenever possible, these friends should learn the importance of delaying the discussion of problems until after the match is over. It is of course the player's responsibility to convey this information to these people. Do not expect that everyone will automatically perceive the world from your viewpoint. You must help them to understand your world and how important concentration is to your success.

Another frequent problem that destroys concentration is the conflict between winning friends and winning tennis matches. There are times when you need to separate the two. If you are overly concerned with what all your friends think of you, your thoughts will often be on them rather than your tennis game. Sometimes your friends will try to take you away from your love of tennis. Some people will do this because they like you and are honestly trying to help you. Others will do so because they don't have the discipline to be like you. You must decide who is truly your friend and who is self-centered.

This problem will become especially important as you experience greater success. Some friends will actually turn against you and see only your negative side. Often this occurs due to a perception by your friends that *you* probably do not want anything to do with them. They fear that *you* have outgrown a need for them now that you are a star. You can prevent this from happening by letting them know that this isn't true and that you cherish their friendship no matter how successful you become. You may in fact need them more now than ever before.

Some people will start wanting to be your friend, simply because you are a champion. This will hold true for members of the same and the opposite sex. You must be prepared to deal with this problem without becoming overly suspicious of everyone. Let yourself get to know new acquaintances under your terms. With time you will learn who is a friend and who is using you to their advantage.

Don't be afraid to take a day off now and then and enjoy having fun with your friends or by yourself. You will need it. Sometimes play tennis with your friends and relax and enjoy their company. They will surely enjoy yours. Occasionally hit your shots and let them enjoy your talents but don't get overly competitive. Try to make sure that they enjoy playing with you. Don't decide to be their teacher, but if they ask for help, give it to them.

If these friends start demanding too much of your time, let them know that your goals in life require that you dedicate a certain amount of time to tennis and that it is very important to you. (The amount of time will depend upon your goals.) Make sure that your friends realize that you value their friendship, but not if it means that you can't attain what you want out of tennis.

Many high-level athletes have found that sharing something intimate and personal with friends helps a relationship. It lets your friends know that you do care about them and are willing to trust them with this intimate feeling. You may wish to discuss your frustrations, or recount particularly anxious or embarrassing situations. But most importantly, you must share with your friends how much tennis means to you. If you wish to get better and better, or merely to enjoy it more, be prepared to share with the other important people in your life.

ONWARD AND UPWARD

You are now ready to embark on a most enjoyable experience—knowing that you can play better tennis, and working systematically toward that goal! You now have a strategy that will help you to find out just how good a tennis player you can become. Get into it and enjoy the process. It is the enjoyment of this process, this search for your limits, that can be so very exciting.

Be sure that as you begin your new approach to tennis you continuously encourage yourself and find ways to feel good about your efforts. If others try to discourage you from believing in yourself, don't listen. Be your own motivator. Believe in yourself and make yourself a successful tennis player.

Do not become the type of tennis player who only focuses on the negative aspects of your tennis game. As mentioned throughout this book, you must work to eliminate your weaknesses—but do not become so obsessed with them that your mental approach to tennis becomes negative. Be good to yourself. Praise your good qualities and look for strengths while working to eliminate weaknesses. Go ahead and be modest and humble when you talk to others, but when you talk to yourself, be confident and praise yourself. Listen to the statements made by the pros, but remember that when they make statements, they are often saying what they think others want them to say. What they say in public is probably not what they say to themselves when it is time to play. You can be sure that they believe in themselves and utilize positive imagery and self-talk.

When it is time for you to perform, dwell on your strengths and feel good about yourself. Look for something good about every point you play. Don't let yourself slip into the bad habit of criticizing yourself after every shot, or imagining the worst before you even hit the ball. Put into practice the positive strategies you have learned in this book. Believe that if you do, you will improve. Do not question your commitment. Give yourself a chance to be successful.

Every night as you go to bed, close your eyes and relax. Reassure yourself that you are on your way to success. You will

control your mind and your body under the stress of competition. If you make a mistake, you will understand why and be able to self-correct so that it won't happen again.

Let your mind wander off to the tennis courts. See and feel yourself playing great tennis. Hit every shot perfectly and enjoy it. Feel good. See yourself serve well, and be in perfect position to return each shot.

You are no longer afraid of the challenges of tennis. You enjoy them. Your strokes are getting better and better. You feel good about yourself and your tennis. You have put in your practice time, and are ready to play each point, both physically and psychologically.

PLAN: PERFORMING AND LEARNING ANALYSIS

1st SERVER	SET # SET SCORE	2nd SERVER

Game 1 ○
Service
Server
Receiver

←○ Game 1
Game 2 ○
Service
Server
Receiver

Game 2 ○→
Game 3 ○
Service
Server
Receiver

←○ Game 3
Game 4 ○
Service
Server
Receiver

Game 4 ○→
Game 5 ○
Service
Server
Receiver

←○ Game 5
Game 6 ○
Service
Server
Receiver

Game 6 ○→
Game 7 ○
Service
Server
Receiver

←○ Game 7
Game 8 ○
Service
Server
Receiver

Game 8 ○→
Game 9 ○
Service
Server
Receiver

←○ Game 9
Game 10 ○
Service
Server
Receiver

Game 10 ○→
Game 11 ○
Service
Server
Receiver

←○ Game 11
Game 12 ○
Service
Server
Receiver

Tie Breaker	○
	○

STROKE ASSESSMENT

Forehand	Backhand	Lob	Overhead	Forehand Volley	Backhand Volley
F	B	L	O	FV	BV
F	B	L	O	FV	BV
F	B	L	O	FV	BV
F	B	L	O	FV	BV
F	B	L	O	FV	BV
F	B	L	O	FV	BV
F	B	L	O	FV	BV
F	B	L	O	FV	BV
F	B	L	O	FV	BV
F	B	L	O	FV	BV
F	B	L	O	FV	BV
F	B	L	O	FV	BV
F	B	L	O	FV	BV
F	B	L	O	FV	BV
F	B	L	O	FV	BV
F	B	L	O	FV	BV
F	B	L	O	FV	BV
F	B	L	O	FV	BV
F	B	L	O	FV	BV
F	B	L	O	FV	BV
F	B	L	O	FV	BV
F	B	L	O	FV	BV
F	B	L	O	FV	BV
F	B	L	O	FV	BV

KEY

☒ = Ace
/ = 1st Serve in
2 = 2nd Serve in
◪ = Double Fault

☒ = Winner of Point
⊗ = Winner of Game

O = Unforced Error
/ = Forced Error
X = Winner!

PLAN: PERFORMING AND LEARNING ANALYSIS

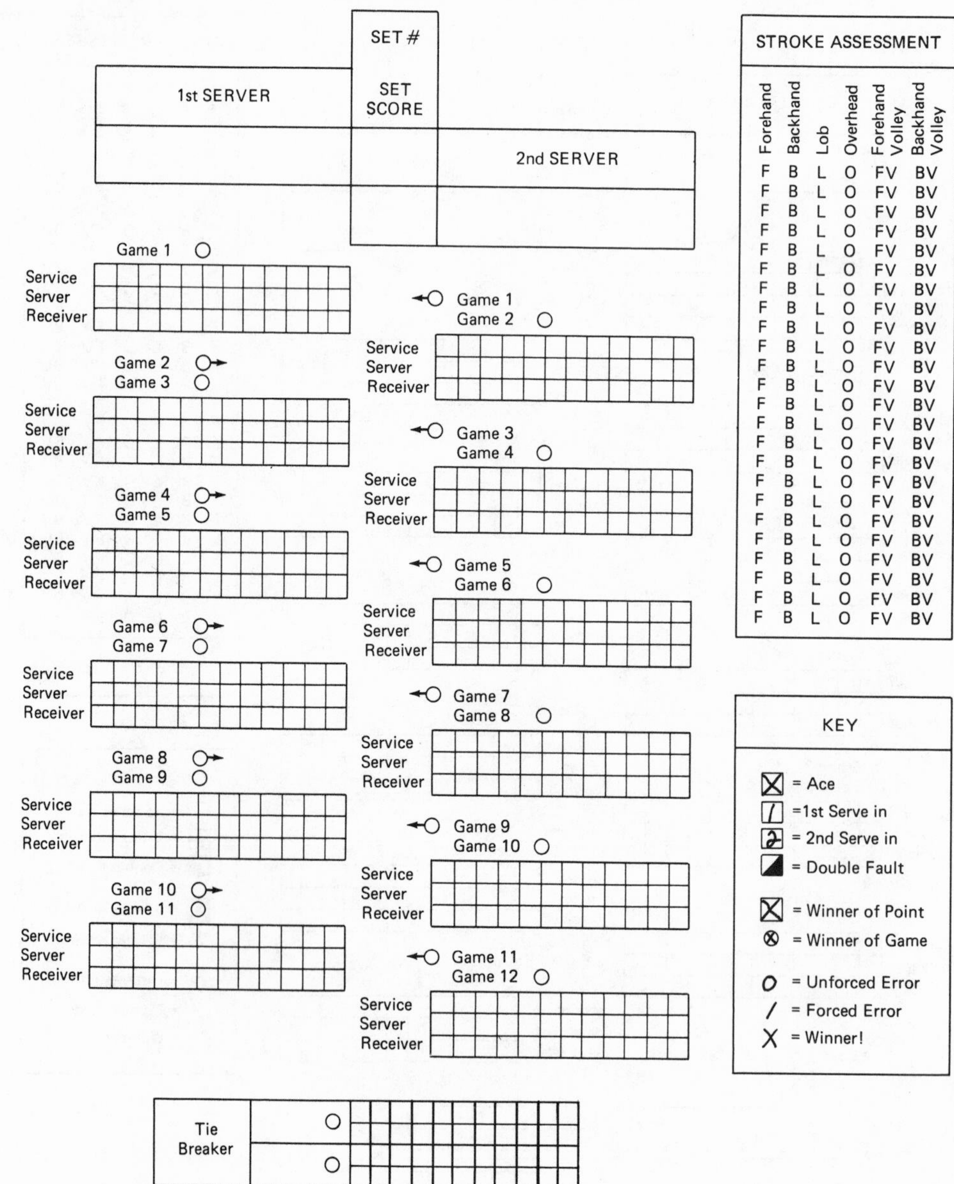

PLAN: PERFORMING AND LEARNING ANALYSIS

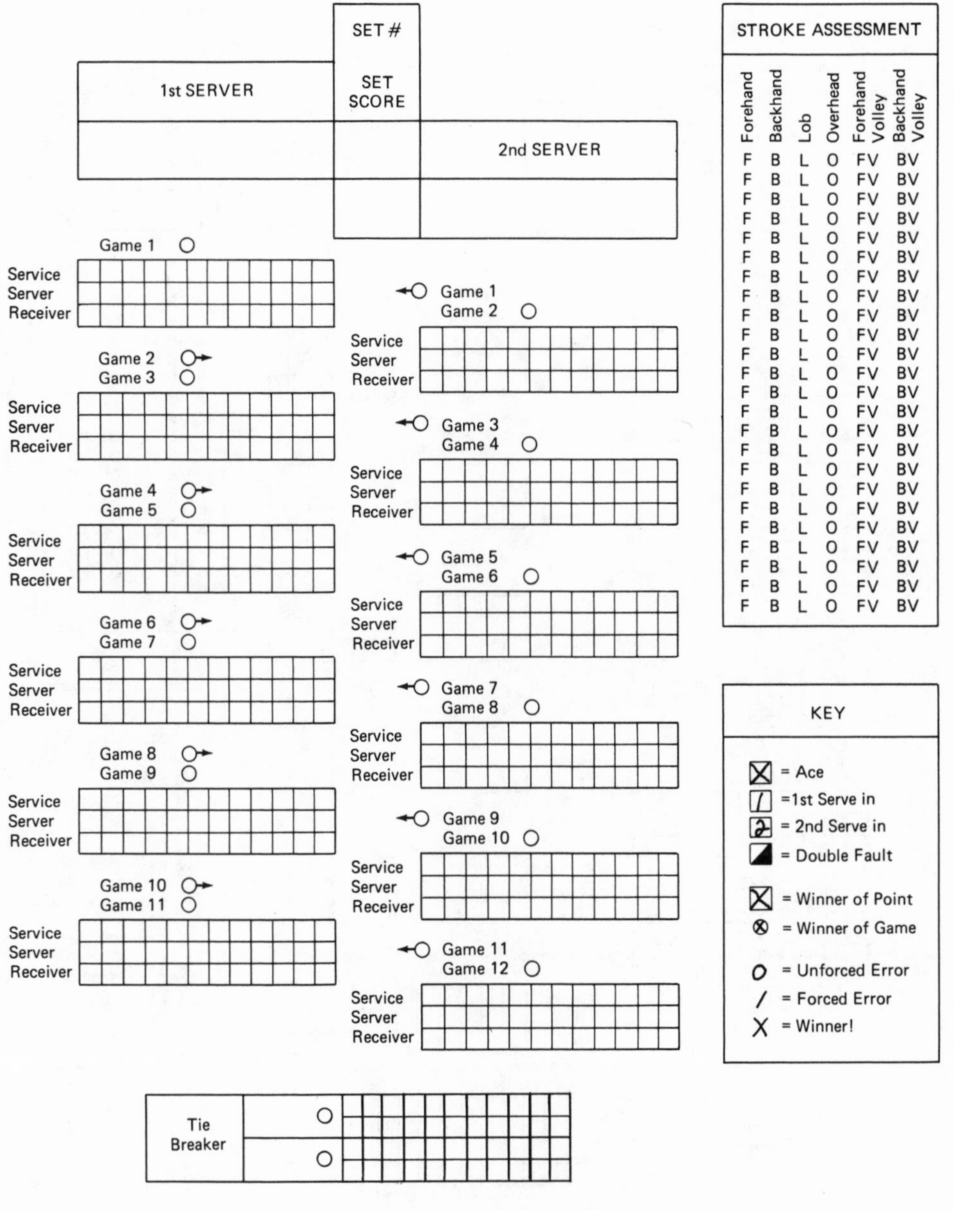

PLAN: PERFORMING AND LEARNING ANALYSIS

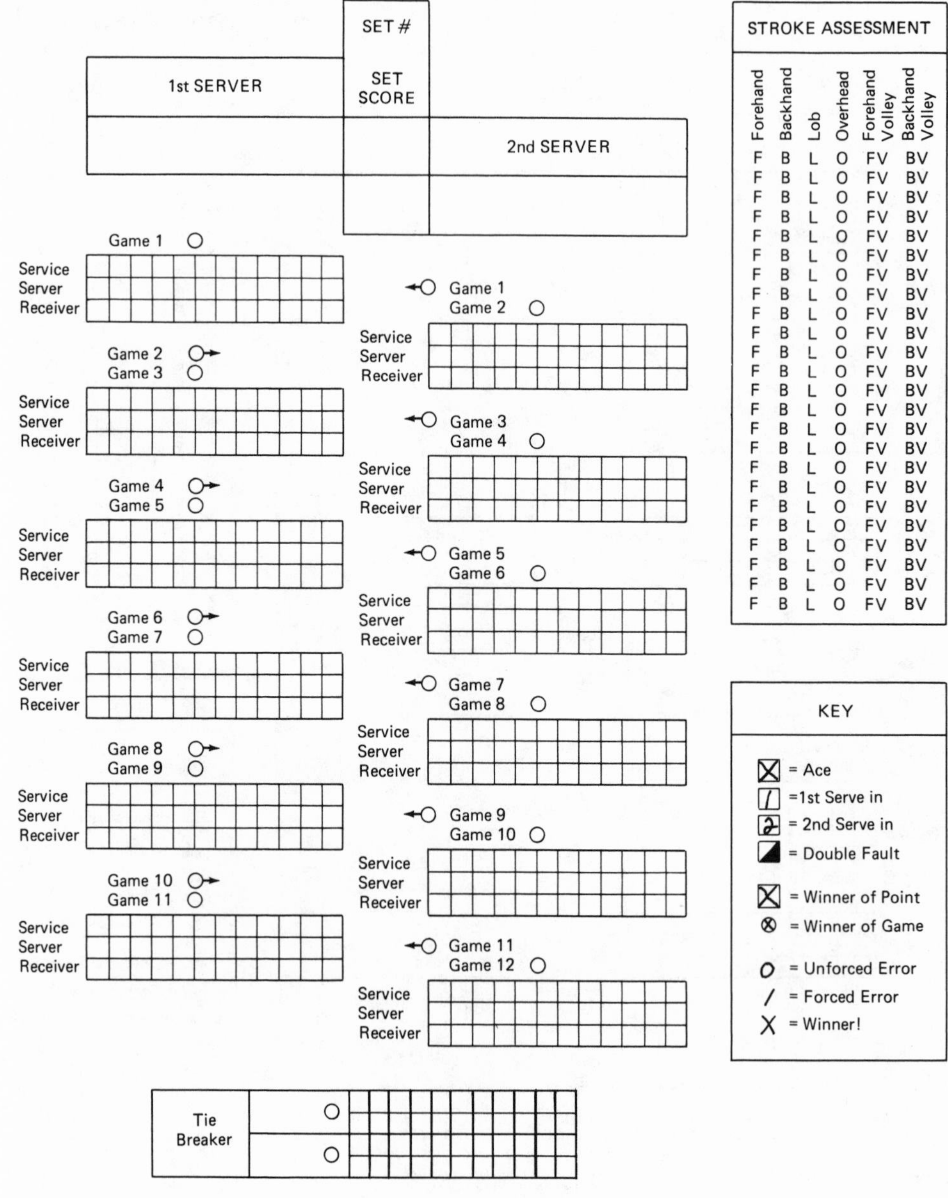

PLAN: PERFORMING AND LEARNING ANALYSIS

1st SERVER	SET # / SET SCORE	2nd SERVER

Game 1

Service
Server
Receiver

Game 2
Game 3

Service
Server
Receiver

Game 4
Game 5

Service
Server
Receiver

Game 6
Game 7

Service
Server
Receiver

Game 8
Game 9

Service
Server
Receiver

Game 10
Game 11

Service
Server
Receiver

Game 1
Game 2

Service
Server
Receiver

Game 3
Game 4

Service
Server
Receiver

Game 5
Game 6

Service
Server
Receiver

Game 7
Game 8

Service
Server
Receiver

Game 9
Game 10

Service
Server
Receiver

Game 11
Game 12

Service
Server
Receiver

STROKE ASSESSMENT					
Forehand	Backhand	Lob	Overhead	Forehand Volley	Backhand Volley
F	B	L	O	FV	BV
F	B	L	O	FV	BV
F	B	L	O	FV	BV
F	B	L	O	FV	BV
F	B	L	O	FV	BV
F	B	L	O	FV	BV
F	B	L	O	FV	BV
F	B	L	O	FV	BV
F	B	L	O	FV	BV
F	B	L	O	FV	BV
F	B	L	O	FV	BV
F	B	L	O	FV	BV
F	B	L	O	FV	BV
F	B	L	O	FV	BV
F	B	L	O	FV	BV
F	B	L	O	FV	BV
F	B	L	O	FV	BV
F	B	L	O	FV	BV
F	B	L	O	FV	BV
F	B	L	O	FV	BV
F	B	L	O	FV	BV
F	B	L	O	FV	BV
F	B	L	O	FV	BV
F	B	L	O	FV	BV

KEY

☒ = Ace
☐ = 1st Serve in
☐ = 2nd Serve in
◪ = Double Fault

☒ = Winner of Point
⊗ = Winner of Game

O = Unforced Error
/ = Forced Error
X = Winner!

Tie Breaker

PLAN: PERFORMING AND LEARNING ANALYSIS

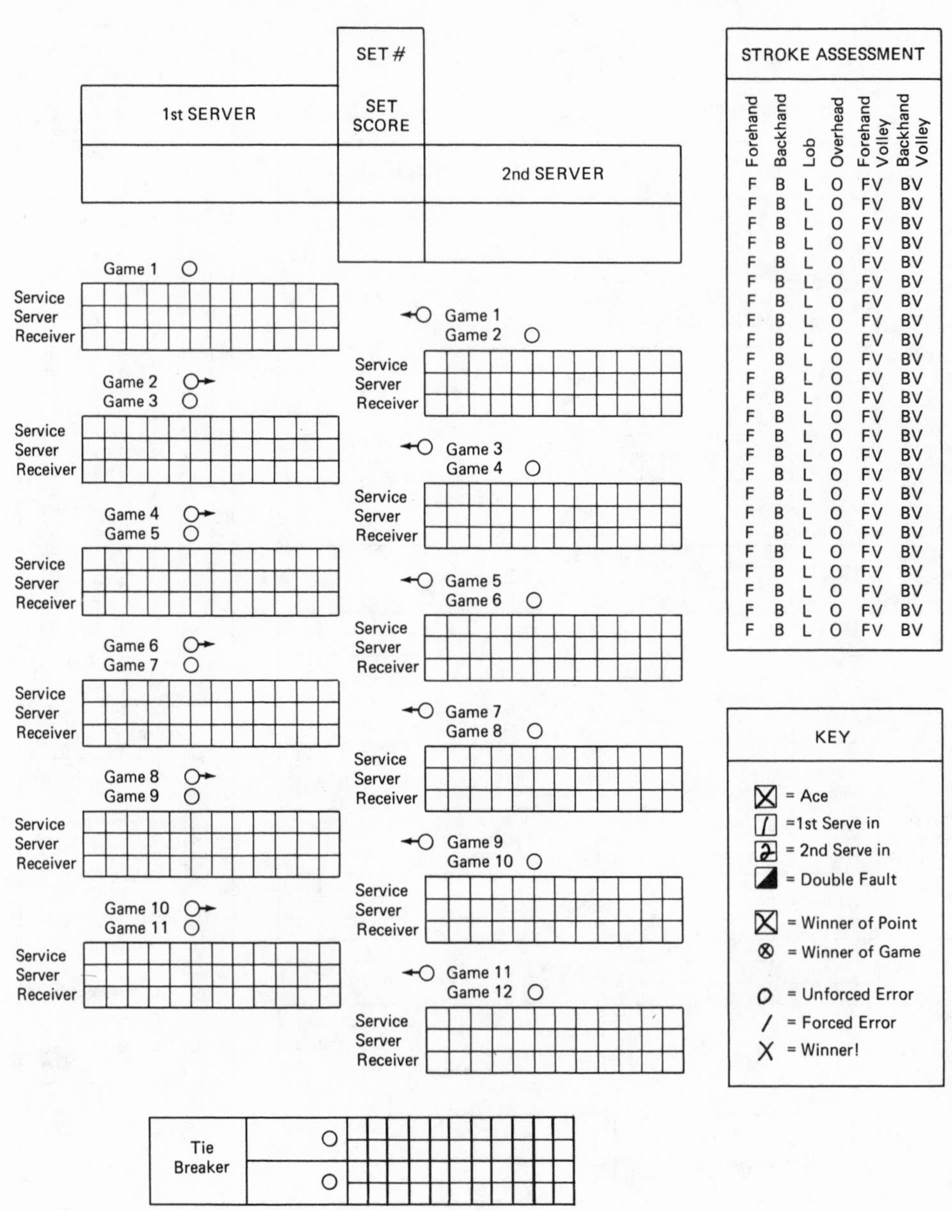

PLAN: PERFORMING AND LEARNING ANALYSIS

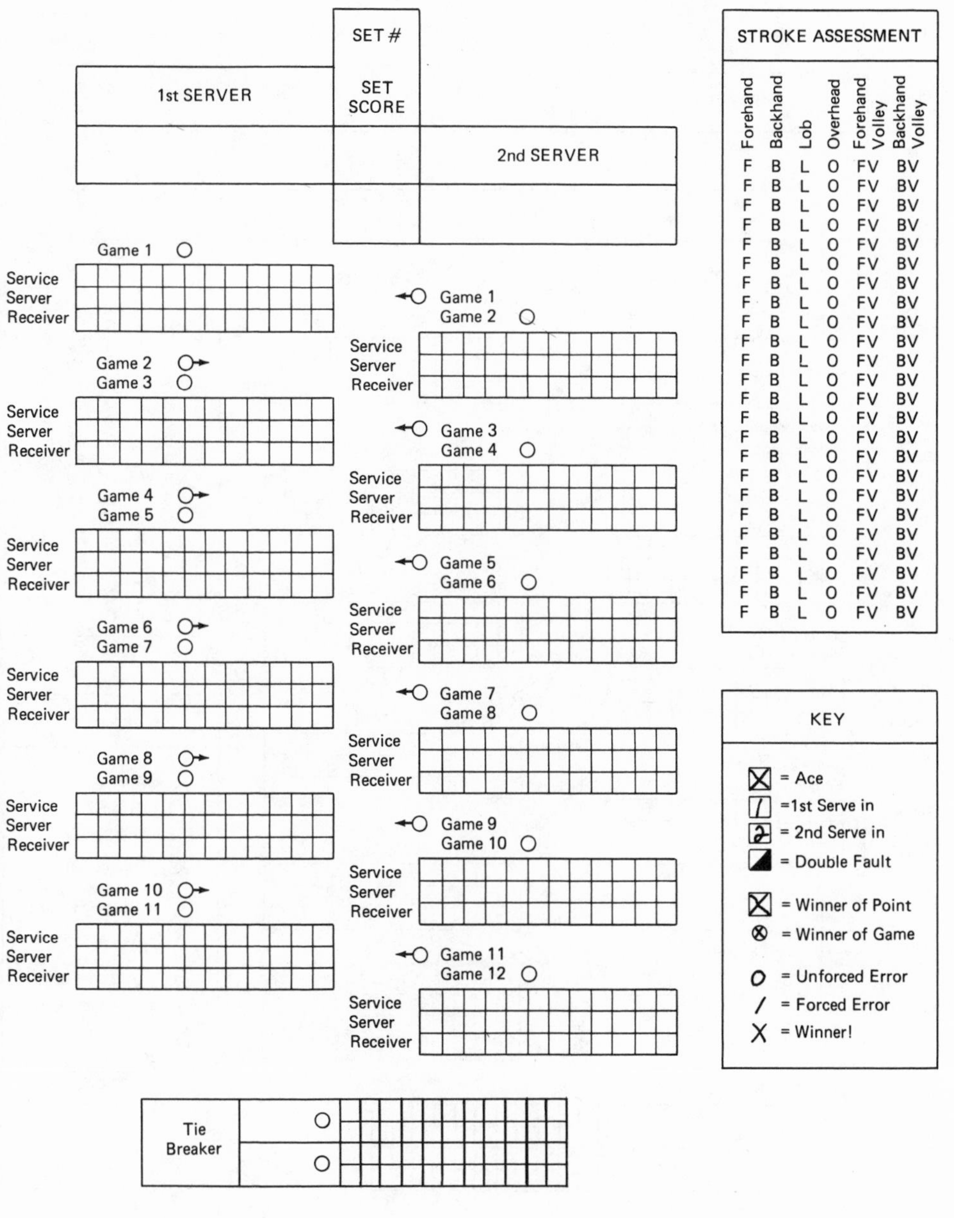

PLAN: PERFORMING AND LEARNING ANALYSIS

1st SERVER	SET # / SET SCORE	2nd SERVER

1st Server

Game 1 ○
Service / Server / Receiver

Game 2 ○→
Game 3 ○
Service / Server / Receiver

Game 4 ○→
Game 5 ○
Service / Server / Receiver

Game 6 ○→
Game 7 ○
Service / Server / Receiver

Game 8 ○→
Game 9 ○
Service / Server / Receiver

Game 10 ○→
Game 11 ○
Service / Server / Receiver

2nd Server

←○ Game 1
Game 2 ○
Service / Server / Receiver

←○ Game 3
Game 4 ○
Service / Server / Receiver

←○ Game 5
Game 6 ○
Service / Server / Receiver

←○ Game 7
Game 8 ○
Service / Server / Receiver

←○ Game 9
Game 10 ○
Service / Server / Receiver

←○ Game 11
Game 12 ○
Service / Server / Receiver

Tie Breaker	
	○
	○

STROKE ASSESSMENT

Forehand	Backhand	Lob	Overhead	Forehand Volley	Backhand Volley
F	B	L	O	FV	BV
F	B	L	O	FV	BV
F	B	L	O	FV	BV
F	B	L	O	FV	BV
F	B	L	O	FV	BV
F	B	L	O	FV	BV
F	B	L	O	FV	BV
F	B	L	O	FV	BV
F	B	L	O	FV	BV
F	B	L	O	FV	BV
F	B	L	O	FV	BV
F	B	L	O	FV	BV
F	B	L	O	FV	BV
F	B	L	O	FV	BV
F	B	L	O	FV	BV
F	B	L	O	FV	BV
F	B	L	O	FV	BV
F	B	L	O	FV	BV
F	B	L	O	FV	BV
F	B	L	O	FV	BV
F	B	L	O	FV	BV
F	B	L	O	FV	BV
F	B	L	O	FV	BV
F	B	L	O	FV	BV

KEY

[☒] = Ace
[/] = 1st Serve in
[2] = 2nd Serve in
[◪] = Double Fault

[☒] = Winner of Point
⊗ = Winner of Game

O = Unforced Error
/ = Forced Error
X = Winner!

PLAN: PERFORMING AND LEARNING ANALYSIS

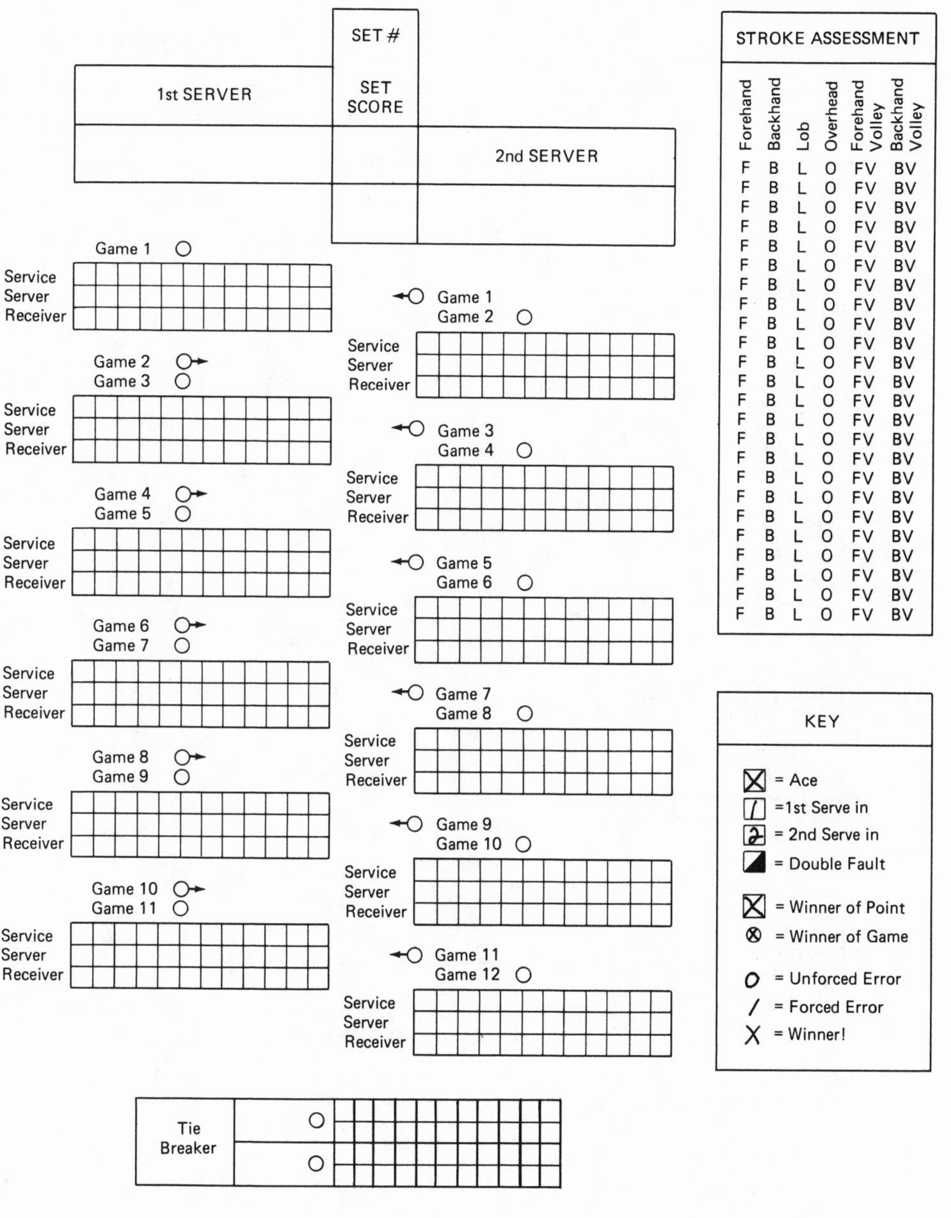

1st SERVER	SET # / SET SCORE	2nd SERVER

Game 1
Service / Server / Receiver

Game 1
Game 2
Service / Server / Receiver

Game 2
Game 3
Service / Server / Receiver

Game 3
Game 4
Service / Server / Receiver

Game 4
Game 5
Service / Server / Receiver

Game 5
Game 6
Service / Server / Receiver

Game 6
Game 7
Service / Server / Receiver

Game 7
Game 8
Service / Server / Receiver

Game 8
Game 9
Service / Server / Receiver

Game 9
Game 10
Service / Server / Receiver

Game 10
Game 11
Service / Server / Receiver

Game 11
Game 12
Service / Server / Receiver

Tie Breaker

STROKE ASSESSMENT

Forehand	Backhand	Lob	Overhead	Forehand Volley	Backhand Volley
F	B	L	O	FV	BV
F	B	L	O	FV	BV
F	B	L	O	FV	BV
F	B	L	O	FV	BV
F	B	L	O	FV	BV
F	B	L	O	FV	BV
F	B	L	O	FV	BV
F	B	L	O	FV	BV
F	B	L	O	FV	BV
F	B	L	O	FV	BV
F	B	L	O	FV	BV
F	B	L	O	FV	BV
F	B	L	O	FV	BV
F	B	L	O	FV	BV
F	B	L	O	FV	BV
F	B	L	O	FV	BV
F	B	L	O	FV	BV
F	B	L	O	FV	BV
F	B	L	O	FV	BV
F	B	L	O	FV	BV
F	B	L	O	FV	BV
F	B	L	O	FV	BV
F	B	L	O	FV	BV
F	B	L	O	FV	BV

KEY

= Ace
=1st Serve in
= 2nd Serve in
= Double Fault
= Winner of Point
= Winner of Game
= Unforced Error
= Forced Error
= Winner!

PLAN: PERFORMING AND LEARNING ANALYSIS

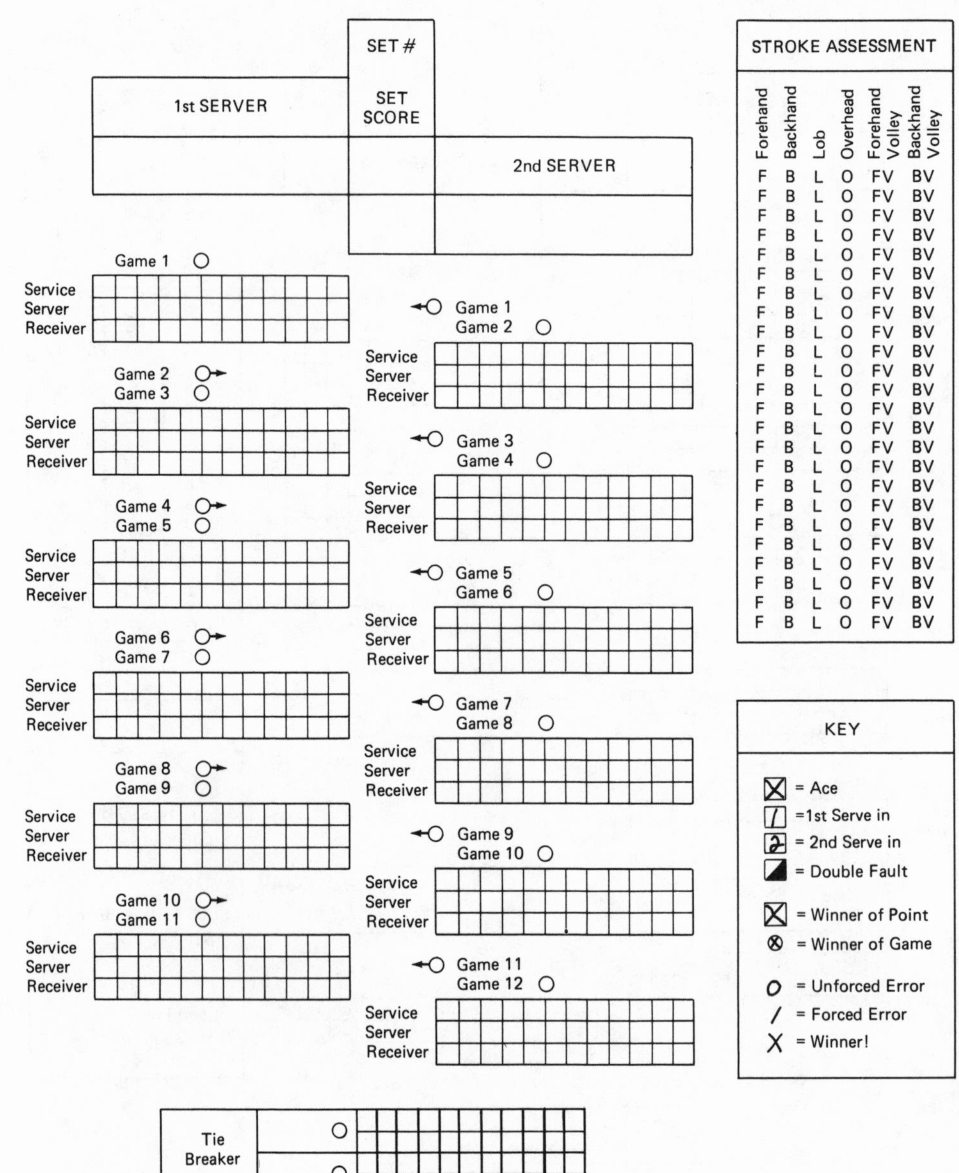

Tie Breaker

Index